MILLENNIUM
PROPHECIES

OTHER BOOKS BY MARK THURSTON

The Edgar Cayce Handbook for Creating Your Future (coauthor)
The Great Teachings of Edgar Cayce
Soul Purpose: Discovering and Fulfilling Your Destiny
Dreams: Tonight's Answers for Tomorrow's Questions
Slow Down and Simplify Your Life
Attain Peace, Surrender Fear
Paradox of Power
The Inner Power of Silence
Discovering Your Soul's Purpose
How to Interpret Your Dreams
Understand and Develop Your ESP
Experiments in Practical Spirituality
Experiments in a Search for God
Meditation and the Mind of Man (coauthor)
Synchronicity as Spiritual Guidance

MILLENNIUM PROPHECIES

*Predictions for the
Coming Century
from Edgar Cayce*

MARK THURSTON, PH.D.

KENSINGTON BOOKS
http://www.kensingtonbooks.com

The author gratefully acknowledges permission from Harcourt Brace & Company to reprint a passage from *Modern Man in Search of a Soul* by C. G. Jung.

Edgar Cayce Readings copyrighted Edgar Cayce Foundation © 1971, 1993, 1994, 1995, 1996. All rights reserved. Used by permission.

KENSINGTON BOOKS are published by

Kensington Publishing Corp.
850 Third Avenue
New York, NY 10022

ISBN 1-57566-143-8

First Printing: July, 1997
10 9 8 7 6 5

Printed in the United States of America

Contents

Chapter 1

THE MESSAGE OF A MODERN-DAY PROPHET

E dgar Cayce sat on the edge of a couch in his study. As he loosened his shirt collar, he looked at his wife Gertrude sitting in a chair just a few feet away. It was 11:30 in the morning in late June of 1936. Out of the corner of his eye, Cayce caught the movement of a duck on the pond of Lake Holly, which bordered the backyard of his home in Virginia Beach. On a day like this, he would almost rather be sitting out on his pier fishing than preparing to do a psychic reading for the five thousandth time.

But this was to be no ordinary psychic reading, if in fact there was any such thing as "ordinary" in Cayce's daily work as a clairvoyant and spiritual counselor. What made this day remarkable was the contents of a piece of paper in Gertrude's hand—a record of one of the most amazing dreams Edgar Cayce himself had ever experienced. Today they planned to get an interpretation of this dream—an interpretation that would come from Cayce's own higher mind, or superconscious. They would ask if the fantastic and even frightening vision that had come to Cayce in the night not long ago was actually a literal prophecy of events in the next two hundred years.

Every word that he would speak during the entranced reading

would be stenographically recorded by his secretary, Gladys Davis, who sat alongside Gertrude. Since 1923 Gladys had been practically a member of the Cayce family, present for every reading and always preparing a permanent, typed copy of the reading from her shorthand notes. The three of them now began a sequence they had followed thousands of times. First was a period of prayer together. Cayce had always understood his capacity to give clairvoyant and prophetic information as an outgrowth of his devotional life. This was *not* a freakish gift that had descended upon him magically at age twenty-three. Instead, he knew this rare talent to be the direct result of his commitment to God's work; it was an intuitive sensitivity that needed constant renewal from his prayer life.

Immediately after this silent, devotional period, Cayce lay back on his couch. Maintaining the focused frame of mind that prayer had created, he placed his hands over his forehead and let himself relax deeper and deeper. After a minute, a bright white light began to emerge from his inner field of vision—a sign to him that he was now ready to begin to draw insight and understanding from his superconscious mind. As an indicator to Gertrude and Gladys, he moved his hands down to his solar plexus, where they would remain folded for the next half an hour. To anyone who didn't know better, he now looked like a middle-aged man lying on his back taking a midday nap.

These movements, however, were a sign to Gertrude that he was ready to receive a hypnoticlike suggestion, directing him to allow certain information to come forth. Today she asked for information to better understand and interpret various psychic and spiritual experiences of Cayce's, especially his extraordinary dream.

After a short time of silence in the room, Edgar Cayce began to speak. For about ten minutes he presented a lesson about psychic perception. This discourse contained principles about how Cayce in the months and years ahead could get the best quality information from his talent. There was a reminder about the motives and ideals that would continue to allow his gift to express itself: *a commitment to service.* As he said in this opening discourse, it was "for the most part for a universal service, or the thought of the others rather than self."

At the conclusion of this opening discourse, the entranced Cayce invited specific questions, and Gertrude asked for an interpretation of the very special dream that had come to Edgar Cayce several weeks earlier. At face value it seemed to predict cataclysmic changes for the earth over the next two hundred years.

In the dream Cayce saw himself as a child. He realized that he had been reincarnated and the date was 2158. His hometown was in Nebraska, but with a very different setting than we know in the twentieth century. Nebraska was now along a seacoast.

As this child, he had conscious recollection of having been Edgar Cayce two centuries earlier. His insistence about this memory drew to him a group of scientists who wanted to check out the boy's claims. The scientists had long beards, scant hair, and wore thick glasses. They decided that the best way to confirm or invalidate his assertion was to take him to some of the places where he remembered having lived or worked before: Kentucky, Alabama, New York, Michigan, and of course, Virginia. To get to these sites they traveled in "a long, cigar-shaped, metal flying ship which moved at high speed."

As they made this multistop journey, the dreaming Cayce observed amazing changes to the geography of America. Water covered parts of Alabama. The Atlantic Ocean city of Norfolk had grown tremendously and now included an immense port facility. Even more dramatic, New York City was in the process of being rebuilt. He could not tell if the destruction had come from warfare or an earthquake.

Through his travels, Cayce also saw changes in the way people lived. Industries were not so centralized, but instead scattered across the countryside. And people resided in homes largely made of glass.

In this dream, the scientists were successful in finding records of the work of this man Edgar Cayce who had lived more than two hundred years earlier. The group gathered up these records and took them back to Nebraska for further study. Then the dream had ended.

When Gertrude finished reading the dream, there was a long pause. Then the entranced Cayce began to speak, offering an interpretation. The meaning of the dream was two-fold. First, it was a promise. It was encouragement to him, saying "Your work will be remembered. Even two hundred years from now it will be possible to find records of your work. It won't be lost."

This was significant because the dream had occurred on a train ride back to Virginia Beach after a disastrous trip to Detroit. During his short stay in Michigan, Cayce had been thrown in jail for practicing medicine without a license—for giving psychic readings with diagnostic, clairvoyant information for sick people. Thousands of times before, these health readings had been given in Virginia and elsewhere, and with great success. But they seemed mysterious and suspicious in Detroit, and he was arrested. There had been an embarrassing courtroom trial before he was finally released and allowed to return to his home state.

The episode had truly been one of the most depressing, discouraging points in Cayce's life. It made him wonder if this work to which he had devoted most of his adult life was ever going to be appreciated. Had it all ultimately been in vain? Then, sleeping on the train headed back to Virginia, this encouraging dream had come.

The second meaning of the dream was literally prophetic; the specifics of the vision would come to pass. In fact, the geography of America could be expected to change exactly as seen in this experience. The ways of life that he had briefly glimpsed in this dream would actually transpire. Making reference to an enigmatic biblical passage about the timeliness for transformation (i.e., ". . . the times and half times"), Cayce announced: "These changes in the earth will come to pass, for the time and times and half times are at an end, and there begin those periods for the readjustments. For how hath He given? 'The righteous shall inherit the earth.'"

When the reading came to an end, Gertrude gave her husband another hypnoticlike suggestion, this time to come back to normal, waking consciousness. Slowly he began to stir. Then he opened his eyes, moved about a bit on the couch and finally sat up. As was always the case, he remembered nothing of what he had said. His last memory was seeing the white light and feeling himself become more and more relaxed. Now he had awakened and the reading was over. He learned the content of what he had just uttered only by Gladys reading it back to him from her stenographic notes.

Times of Change

Cayce marveled for many months at the reading he had given that summer morning in 1936. He wasn't surprised that it spoke literally of drastic changes to come in the world. On several earlier occasions he had given prophetic readings, and there would be many more in the next eight years. But no Cayce prophecy before or after that morning in 1936 would speak so specifically about the world two centuries hence.

In many ways predictions about troubled times in the decades and centuries ahead were a match to the conditions of Cayce's own world of the mid-1930s. It was a time of uncertainty and distress. The world was still in the throes of an awful economic depression—something that Cayce's own readings had warned of before the 1929 Stock Market crash. In April 1929, Cayce told one man of the very real probability that "there must surely come a break where it would be *panic* in the money centers—not *only* of Wall Street's activity but a closing of the boards in many centers . . ." (#137–117 in the Cayce files).

Wars and rumors of wars were in the air, and the greatest international conflagration in history loomed only a few years ahead—again, something that Cayce had clairvoyantly seen coming in 1935 with these prophetic words: "This will make for the taking of sides, as it were, by various groups or countries or governments.

This will be indicated by the Austrians, Germans, and later the Japanese joining in their influence.... For these will gradually make for a growing of animosities. And unless there is interference from what may be called by many the *supernatural* forces and influences that are activative in the affairs of nations and peoples, the whole *world*, as it were, will be set on fire by the militaristic groups and those that are for power and expansion . . ." (#416–7).

But in the world that would finally emerge from the Great Depression and World War II, there would be still greater changes yet to be met, according to the Cayce predictions. The turn of the millennium would signify an even more drastic metamorphosis. There was yet to come geological and geographic transformation, and perhaps even more significant, *consciousness changes* that would usher in the next one thousand years.

In fact, we are in the midst of those changes right now. The signs are all around us: We live in a world of instability among nations. Our international economic system continually demonstrates its precariousness and uncertainty. In many ways the social fabric seems to be coming apart. There are almost as many divorces as marriages. Crime is continually on the increase—not only among the disadvantaged, but among the privileged as well. And there are signs all around us that the earth itself is dying, slowly being killed by humanity's mistreatment of the soil, air, water and wildlife of the planet.

Fortunately these signs of destructive change in the world around us are accompanied by many *hopeful* portents. For example, medical science has made tremendous breakthroughs in our capacity to treat otherwise catastrophic illnesses. A worldwide communications network now links the people of the earth in a way unimaginable even fifty years ago. And there is clear evidence of an emerging segment of society that holds a holistic vision of human nature and ways of living. But even these creative, positive signs of change still leave us with the challenges and stresses of living in a world that is continually and rapidly altering.

The signs of turmoil and change are not just outward ones.

Perhaps even more important are those changes going on *within people.* We know these signs very well; unfortunately most are known to us because of the difficulties they create. There has been a tremendous increase in stress-related physical illnesses. To a large measure the problems of high blood pressure, heart disease and cancer can probably be traced to the tensions of living in a world that is changing so quickly.

Almost all of us are more likely than ever before to feel hurried and pushed. It's a natural inner response to a world that seems to demand, "Get things done now before conditions change again and the opportunity is lost." It's frustrating and demoralizing to know that the quality of our lives could improve if we weren't so rushed. A subtle yet profound kind of pessimism has emerged. For some people the sense of hopelessness comes from a feeling of frustration that nothing will ever be done about their disadvantaged situation. For others there is pessimism because it is so difficult to plan reliably for an uncertain future and build any sense of security.

What does it mean to live in these times of change? Do all of these signs of decay make it a cursed period of history? Or is it rather a blessing to have been born in such a time of transition? Perhaps, if we can awaken a courageous and creative spirit within, we will see that this truly is an exciting time to be alive.

But even if we adopt the more hopeful view of what's going on around us and within us, we're left to face the challenge of actually living in these years of the millennium transition. We'll have to learn to cope with stresses that are different from those ever faced by our ancestors. Certainly they had to deal with adversities— many just as difficult as those we face now. In fact, it should lift our spirits about our own times to observe how past generations have made it through their own challenges. Nevertheless, the fact remains that the problems of dealing with a world that changes *as fast* as ours does has never before been met by humanity. How will we cope with this sort of adversity?

One eloquent spokesman of our times succinctly described the many challenges we face as the new millennium approaches. Dr.

Carl Rogers, a pioneer in modern counseling techniques and human-istic psychology, defined the greatest problem facing humanity today: difficulty in dealing with change. At a conference in San Francisco in 1968, entitled "U.S.A.: 2000," Dr. Rogers had this to say about the challenge of living in times of change:

"It is not the hydrogen bomb, fearful as that may be. It is not the population explosion, though the consequences of that are awful to contemplate. It is instead a problem which is rarely mentioned or discussed. It is the question of how much change the human being can accept, absorb, and assimilate, and the rate at which he can take it. Can he keep up with the ever-increasing rate of technological change, or is there some point at which the human organism goes to pieces? Can he leave the static ways and static guidelines which have dominated all of his history, and adopt the process ways, the continual changingness, which must be his if he is to survive?"

The primary purpose of this book is to make a creative contribu-tion to meeting the very test Dr. Rogers has described. The approach is threefold: to provide hope, understanding and creative alternatives. First we need a perspective of hopefulness, for with-out a sense of positive possibilities it is very hard for us to make it through adversity. By analogy, without a clear vision of a fulfilling vocation, a student is unlikely to make it through the stresses of higher education. Without a feeling of promise for the fruits of his labors, a gardener or farmer will not find strength to tend the soil and crops. Human beings need the feeling of promise in order to unleash the creative, spiritual energies that make us unique.

And there is much to be hopeful about. Although the final out-come is not assured, there are strong possibilities that this period of rapid change is part of a birthing process—that a spiritually renewed earth and humanity is about to emerge. Many sources of information, including the Edgar Cayce millennium prophecies, offer us a promise beyond the troubled times in which we live. They say that the pain and stress we feel is a result of the old ways dying so that a new vision of life can be born and lived.

The second aspect of this book's approach is understanding. Much of the stress and trouble created by living in these times of change is because we don't understand what's going on around us. Failing to understand a purpose for what we observe and feel, we easily resort to a state of despair. However, an understanding of what has happened and what's likely to occur soon is an attainable aspiration. The Cayce readings and many other psychics, social scientists and spiritual leaders can provide us with insights to help us grasp the meaning of our times.

And a final element of this book is to propose creative options—meaningful contributions to the future world in which we would like to live. With an ideal clearly in mind—with a sense of spiritual purpose—we can make use of the vast creative abilities available to us. *We need not passively await the future.* A key purpose of this book is to give you a feeling of being empowered, to remind you of the many alternatives and methods available if you wish to be among the builders of a new millennium.

I'm keeping in mind a certain image as I write, a symbolic image that catches the understanding and spirit I hope to sustain about these times of change. It came to me years ago as a dream—one that was a response from my inner self to deep questioning I had about the world in which I found myself. I was discouraged, having lost the feelings of hope, promise and expectancy that had been mine earlier when I first read about a new millennium being born. In that initial encounter with the idea of an emergent new world, I had felt a sort of "mission" to be a contributor to its creation. And for many months, perhaps several years, I had carried inside me an enthusiasm and hope about a coming new planetary culture which I felt sure was just ahead. But now much of that feeling of promise and expectancy had dissipated. I was certainly still on the spiritual path as an individual, and even trying to help others around me with their growth. But the world in which I lived seemed just as deeply in the old ways and old values as ever before.

Despite the discouraging outward signs, I realized how much I missed the enthusiasm and expectancy I had once had. I began to pray regularly about my concern and asked that I might understand both what was going on in the world and what had been going on inside me. The dream that came soon thereafter has been a powerful image in my thinking ever since. Mine was not a vision of specific geographic changes as Edgar Cayce's 1936 prophetic dream had been. Instead it was a symbolic picture of how we as individuals may experience the changes of the millennium shift.

In my dream I was aboard a commercial airline flight. Everything seemed to be going quite normally when suddenly there was an announcement over the loudspeaker. The pilot said that we were about to fly higher than a plane had ever flown before. We were asked to be sure our seat belts were pulled tightly. In the dream there was a tremendous amount of enthusiasm and excitement among all of the passengers (the same sort of excitement I had felt years earlier when I first read of Edgar Cayce's millennium prophecies). I was pleased to have a window seat so that I could view what was going to happen. But as I looked out of the window for the next several minutes, it appeared that nothing changed. We seemed to continue to fly about five thousand feet above the ground. My fellow passengers began to mumble and complain, "What was he talking about? We aren't flying any higher than before."

Then, one of the passengers said he thought he knew what was going on: We were flying up the side of a mountain, staying about five thousand feet off the face of the mountain slope. He predicted, "I bet that soon we'll reach the top of the mountain, break free of it, and we'll see how far up we have really come." And sure enough, as I looked out of my window, the top of the mountain suddenly appeared, and I could see that we were *hundreds of thousands of feet* in the air! And then, the plane disappeared. We were flying by ourselves, and there was a tremendous feeling of exhilaration.

At the time I had this dream, it helped me to understand what might be going on in the world. And it has continued to serve as a potent metaphor to help me deal with the ever-present signs that the old world and the old ways of living are still very much with us. To have looked out the window of the plane and to have seen that we were still just five thousand feet off the ground is much the same experience as watching the evening news or reading the newspaper. The signs so strongly appear to be saying that we have not lifted consciousness in our culture in any significant way. The emergence of a new world order seems like a promise that is not going to be fulfilled.

But as in my dream, things *are* changing. Consciousness is being lifted, but in a way that is not always apparent. The time will likely come when we will suddenly see what inner progress and change has been going on. At that time we will need to become full participants in the changes that have happened. In a spiritual sense we will need to demonstrate our capacity to "fly"—that is, our ability to claim our creative powers and use them wisely.

Edgar Cayce's Definition of the New Millennium

One principle runs like a thread through the entire body of Cayce's psychic work: It's a great privilege to be alive in these times at the change of the millennium. As stressful and difficult as changing times invariably will be, this is an extraordinary moment in human history. Collectively we stand on the threshold of a wonderful opportunity. Each of us has a chance to have a significant effect that will profoundly influence the human family and planet Earth for generations, even centuries, to come.

Although Cayce himself used this phrase only infrequently, we have the chance to move into a "new age." The switch to such a new era is at least as great as the transition five hundred years ago as the Middle Ages faded away and the Renaissance began. It's a privilege to live in these years right before and right after the turn of the millennium because it coincides with a possible transformation of planetary culture. And in his thousands of readings to ordinary and extraordinary people, Cayce documented his philosophy for living in a world going through radical transitions.

Let's examine some of the features and characteristics of the emerging new millennium, as Cayce saw it.

The first feature is *limits*. Whenever things begin to change, we confront barriers. Meeting new limits is a signpost to announce that change is coming. For example, each of us has encountered this principle (or we will some day) as our bodies grow older. It's dismaying to discover at age thirty that you can't short-change yourself on sleep the way you did in your college years. It's startling to realize upon entering middle age that you really do need to get bifocals. The list of examples related to physical health is nearly endless. And the same phenomenon can be observed in other parts of our lives. When a relationship is about to end or at least change significantly, the feeling is often one of having reached a wall or limit. The old way of relating doesn't seem to be working anymore. Whenever a phase in any part of our personal lives comes near an end, the existence of new barriers and obstacles comes into focus.

The same process happens on a broader scale. In readings given for thousands of people, Cayce described how our society is being challenged to change. And with the dimming of the familiar and traditional ways of our culture there comes the experience of *limits*.

In our times we are experiencing the limits of physical consciousness. Like an embryonic chick straining against the confines of the egg's shell, our culture is pressing against the boundaries of the old world ways. To transcend those limits will be a birth into something new for humanity.

In these days of testing and confusing changes, we find ourselves to be *time bound*. Our lives are too full of things that have to be done right away. We're often frustrated that we can't give the needed attention to produce the quality results of which we're capable. Our society is also experiencing at a mass level the condition of being *energy bound*. For example, America is dependent upon imported petroleum, and once every decade or so an international crisis makes us painfully aware of how hemmed in we are by this situation.

What's more, as we confront the limits of physical consciousness, we find the most significant boundary: feeling *power bound*. Frequently people feel powerless to do anything to solve chronic problems—whether it's AIDS, violent crime, the threat of inflation, the rising incidence of divorce or other difficulties facing us.

A second feature of the emerging millennium is that paradoxically it's yet to come *and* it's already here. At a deep level, the essential problem of our times is that we are living in a new world with old world rules. Technology has *already* made us one world. Because of nuclear weapons, global warfare is unthinkable. Because of international trade in the raw materials needed for industry, worldwide cooperation is *already* a necessity. And because of communications breakthroughs (such as satellite relay stations), we can no longer claim ignorance of what's happening for any failure on our part to help our troubled brothers and sisters in other parts of the world. In this sense we can honestly say that a new planetary culture has *already* arrived.

However, the world is still being run with the same procedures and ideals as in the past hundreds of years. Feelings of national (or even regional) pride and sovereignty are stronger than feelings of global family. And things won't work well this way. We cannot play a new game with old rules. And the new game is already upon us.

This leads to a third feature of the emerging millennium: the power of individuals to change the world. Humanity faces a *decision* as the calendar changes over to the twenty-first century. It will be a choice of whether or not to allow *the spirit of oneness to guide human affairs* throughout the globe. Cayce emphatically emphasized time after time that that great decision would be made up of millions of little decisions by everyday people doing everyday tasks and meeting commonplace problems. By what rules will we choose to live in the new planetary culture now emerging? What will be our ideals and intentions toward each other?

The jury is still out on these questions. Much of the stress we call living in times of change is created by this tension. A new kind of world is already here, but it's still not clear what rules for living and relating to each other we are going to choose.

Cayce's Vision of a New Millennium

With these features of the emerging millennium in mind, we can carefully look at exactly what Cayce had to say about a new age or new planetary culture.

Only on rare occasions did he specifically use the term "new age"—a phrase that has taken on a somewhat derogatory connotation in recent years because of a linkage to a flighty, ungrounded attitude toward life. But this is hardly what Cayce meant when he used the term. Instead he envisioned a renewed planetary culture with individuals deeply grounded in a moral and spiritual vision of life on earth.

The most detailed and specific instance in which Cayce defined the coming new world was in 1939 for a forty-one-year-old woman (#1602–3 in the Cayce files). She was a student of ancient mystical traditions and asked Cayce to comment on prophecies of a seventeenth century German seer named Jacob Boehme (pronounced Ber-ma). Boehme was, among other things, an expert on astrology and felt that significant changes would come in the late twentieth century when the sun moved from Pisces to Aquarius in its twenty-four-thousand-year progression through the signs of the zodiac. One change would be the reappearance of the legendary lost continent of Atlantis.

Among other questions, the woman wondered specifically when we might expect to see Atlantis. Cayce didn't speak directly to her question about Atlantis. Instead, he spoke in general terms of coming changes on a global scale, and he identified 1998 as the key year of transition. (This particular reading was *not* one in which Cayce offered details about the land masses or the people to be most directly affected by the changes.) On multiple occasions in this prophecy he emphasized that the coming changes would be *gradual* ones and "not a cataclysmic activity in the experience of the earth in this period."

In two further questions submitted by this woman for the same reading, she asked about the significance of an Age of Aquarius. What would it mean in regard to the physical, mental and spiritual development of humanity? And more specifically, why had one mystic referred to this coming era as the "Age of the Lily"?

There was no simple answer to this kind of question, Cayce began. It would be a growing and unfolding matter. But to understand the kind of awareness that it would bring, we must start by looking back at the previous age—the Piscean era. Near the beginning of that age, Christ came. He demonstrated the capacity of a single individual to live in communication with the Creator *and* to follow a Higher Will. The promise was that in times to come each of us might begin to exhibit a similar consciousness. By understanding the meaning of Christ's coming two thousand years ago, we have a clue to the opportunity that now emerges in an Aquarian Age. In essence, human consciousness during the coming age can develop in a way that Cayce described as "the full consciousness of the ability to communicate with or to be aware of the relationships to the Creative Forces and the uses of same in material environs." But a warning comes with this development—or it should be said redevelopment, because in ancient times humans had similar abilities to draw upon the invisible Creative Forces. For example, Cayce states that the prehistoric civilization of Atlantis brought destruction upon itself because those powers were used willfully and selfishly.

Cayce's answer about what it would be like to live in a new world doesn't describe a physical life-style; it defines the kind of consciousness we would have: a full awareness of our ability to communicate with God and with our own higher selves, and the ability to use these higher vibrational expressions of energy in our material lives. We can well imagine the commonplace use of ESP, psychic and spiritual healing, meditation and the like. However, the warning must stay in the backs of our minds. We might just as easily fall prey to the temptations to misuse these heightened powers.

Cayce continued his prophecy about the birth of the new millennium with this crucial pronouncement: Many people will be unaware of what is really going on during this period of transition. Those who understand the meaning of these times will be the people who are willing to accept the idea that there is an invisible spiritual world. These individuals will recognize the reality of Creative Forces—that is, our Divine Creator. They will see how it is possible to make a direct personal connection with those Forces and make use of them purposefully in material life. What's more, a good place for any of us to start making that discovery is to become sensitive to the vibratory influences that subtly exist between one person and another.

Apparently in these times of change there are likely to be many confused people. Only those individuals who are willing to think in terms of the reality of the psychic and spiritual realms will be aware of and understand what is going on in the world around them. In these times of mass confusion and disorientation, they have a great responsibility. Having at least some understanding of the purposes of what is unfolding, they must share this insight in a form that would make sense of these events for other people.

In the final set of prophetic statements made in this reading, Cayce addressed the issue of why this new millennium might be characterized as the "Age of the Lily" and the timing of its arrival. His answer concerning the lily was simple and elegant. The lily is a symbol of purity. That's what it will take for any of us to achieve the consciousness that humanity is destined to attain during the Aquarian Age. Purity of body. Purity of mind and purpose.

In regard to timing, Cayce predicted that we could best understand what was soon to come as a gradual transition. There would be years in which the influences of this coming new planetary culture would begin to affect human affairs, but there would be a lapping over from the previous era into the new one. One key date, however, was proposed: 1998. This will be the year when "we will begin to understand fully."

This set of prophecies given in 1939 beautifully summarizes the Cayce vision of the new millennium. First, it must be a time of greater purity. To be builders of a new world order, we will have to cleanse our bodies as well as our emotional and thinking processes. Most crucially, our purposes will need to be pure. And then, what is required of us is patience. In spite of calendar dates that artificially define a new era to have come, Cayce suggests that there will be a phasing out of the old and a gradual emergence of this new planetary culture. To his prophetic vision, the year 1998 would be every bit as significant as 2000 or 2001. According to this visionary timetable we should expect that times of change will extend well into the twenty-first century. What will particularly characterize the period up to 1998 is the confusion and lack of understanding about these changing times.

Our Response to the Changing Times

What is needed from us is not just lectures, books and other "words" to explain in an intellectual way what the changes are about; we must also *express* in the midst of stressful times qualities such as faith and hope. This is how we can personally catch our own vision of a new age and help to lift others into this perspective.

Cayce said this bluntly to a twenty-seven-year-old woman in 1937 who came to him for help with a physical ailment (#1436–1). Although his reading for her was largely about remedies to heal her body, he also challenged her to catch a bigger vision of the purpose for being healed. He invited her to claim the visions she had already had for herself concerning the future. She had already glimpsed the possibilities for humanity. She had seen the potential for a new age in which people relate to each other and to their Creator in a new way.

In his advice to this woman, Cayce goes on to predict the factor that would be most likely to keep some people from moving into such a new way of life. The reason would be a failure of character—that is, an inability to express particular qualities: faith, hope, patience, kindness, gentleness, and love. Only by awakening those very character traits will our minds open to a higher understanding of the times in which we live.

This is an important point if we're to understand the Cayce prophecies as a whole. They aren't simply about pinpointing where earthquakes will take place. Nor are they merely about a world in which everyone has suddenly started to believe in metaphysical philosophy. Instead, Cayce's essential vision is of a world for the next millennium in which the Christ-like virtues have truly become a way of life.

It's not going to happen overnight. In fact, it will probably take generations, even centuries. But it's the destiny of humanity to live with hope, patience and love as guiding forces. And so, in describing to this twenty-seven-year-old woman a more careful picture of a new millennium—something Cayce believed she had already glimpsed—he characterized it as a time in which people help people so that "they who are weak take hope, they who have faltered gain new courage, they who are disappointed and disheartened gain a new concept of hope that springs eternally within the human breast."

Of course, it's not very easy to live that way in a stressful, busy world that seems to offer few inducements or rewards to help our fellow humans. In a very practical way, what can help us stay in touch with that sense of personal mission? If we really want to be among those who are trying to create this sort of new age, how can we stay connected to this kind of purpose for living?

We all seem to need a way to keep our thoughts and emotions stable and focused when we're buffeted by the winds of change. We need a way to hold on to this heightened purpose in a period of difficult transition. Cayce recommended the use of short statements—so-called affirmations—that can be repeated aloud or silently to maintain our connection with the best that lives within us. Such affirmations can be used in prayer or meditation, but also in the midst of daily life as we simply pause for a moment and silently remember the words.

One woman in particular was given advice by Cayce regarding an affirmation that she could use to help her through the stressful times when the world would be going through so many changes. There is an archetypal quality to these words, which echo a theme from the "serenity prayer" used in Alcoholics Anonymous. They can quicken within each of us a spirit of peace as we participate in the birth of the new millennium. "Thy will be done, O God! And let me find myself content with that I cannot change, and to change that which I may that will be in closer keeping with Thee."

When Will a New Age Come?

The question of timing is always a problem with predictions. It's not only a matter of *what* will happen but also *when*. Some people have grown tired of waiting for the fulfillment of predictions about major world changes. They got their hopes up, believing that tremendous changes were just around the corner, only to get up morning after morning to the same old world. For them, additional information about prophecies is like the story of "The Boy Who Cried 'Wolf.'" They don't want to be tricked yet again. How long *will* it be until we see signs of a new consciousness directing human affairs? Will it be in the years right around 2001? Or is it still hundreds of years off?

The old systems and the old consciousness won't keep on working indefinitely, simply because they sow too many seeds of their own undoing. Some type of major change must be just ahead, and there are four basic scenarios for how a new age could emerge out of the present state of our world.

The first hypothesis is a grim one. It suggests that things will have to get much worse before people will be willing to work together to build something better. This theory presupposes a sort of Dark Ages that would precede renewal. Books like *1984* and *Brave New World* could be included in this first category of scenarios, with their frightful images of modern, technological ideals carried to their absurd and freedom-destroying ultimate.

A second theory is that a spiritually refocused new age society will emerge relatively soon—at least by the early years of the twenty-first century. This scenario is antitechnology and supposes that soon the world will clearly see how a consumer-based culture doesn't work. It predicts that we will turn to a more contemplative alternative which features the individual in harmony with nature and a suspension of scientific development until the spiritual development in humans can catch up.

A third story also imagines that a new age is coming very soon, but this version is protechnology. It suggests that science is going to discover what religion has been asking us to accept on faith. Through science we will find evidence for life after death, for psychic healing and for the value of meditation. There will be a wedding of science and religion which will move us into a new world order. This version predicts that the scientific technological establishment will still be running the world in the twenty-first century, but it will be with new, spiritual values, the rightness of which has been proven.

A fourth theory suggests that it is still hundreds of years away. In this scenario the transition is very gradual. Each generation will make a little more progress. It rests on the assumption that a new age can come only as a reflection of changes in human thinking and ideals, and it points out that humans are slow to change. According to this fourth hypothesis, the seeds are being planted right now—particularly in the last half of the twentieth century— but it will take many generations for these new values to flower in humanity as a whole.

Proponents of each of the theories feel that they can find something in the Cayce prophecies to support their positions. Since Cayce's death in 1945 the majority of those who have studied his predictions feel that the antitechnology theory is most likely. A new age is coming right around the turn of the millennium, and severe earth changes will be the trigger as they undermine our smug overconfidence in human technological prowess. The earth itself will shake our pride and, forcing us to our knees, will make us look for a better way to live on this planet.

However, the majority interpretation does not always prove to be the one that's true. We shouldn't be too quick to dismiss the idea that a new age may be hundreds of years away—at least in the sense of a new age in which all humanity participates. Individuals or groups could enter a new type of consciousness and life-style even now, and *for them* it will be as if a new age is here. But more broadly speaking, humanity must eventually travel *together* in spiritual evolution.

For right now the question of timing cannot be answered. Each of us must decide personally how we will take these prophecies. We must develop for ourselves a perspective of how we build a new world. Are we "sprinters" racing toward the year 2001 and the start of a new millennium; or are we "long-distance runners" who believe that in this lifetime we may not see the fruits of all we are trying to accomplish?

Maybe we can find in the history books certain lessons that show us how humanity passes through major cultural transformation. If we look back at some of the great transition times for humanity, we can see a variety of examples.

One contrast is between the first century A.D. and the conclusion of the Middle Ages. Will our own times of change be more like the years A.D. 30 to A.D. 90 or the years 1490 to 1550? The first is the period of Christ's ministry and the formation of the early Christian Church. The second period was the time of a flowering Renaissance. Looking at the secular history of the world from A.D. 30 to A.D. 90, it appears that nothing of great importance happened. The Romans merely consolidated their hold on all of the known Western world. Seen from this point of view, these sixty years were not particularly times of great transformation and change. However, we can look back on those years from another perspective and see that they really were the beginning of a new age. A relatively small group of people went through a quantum jump in consciousness. However, it took hundreds of years for that experience to be recognized and accepted by the mainstream culture in which they lived.

Is this what is happening in our own time? Perhaps once again a relatively small group of people are going through a different but equally important quantum jump in the evolution of consciousness. This time it may be hundreds of thousands of people, whereas in the first century it was only thousands. But the pattern may be the same: it may take many years for society as a whole to be affected.

However, this isn't the only pattern for changing times. It may be that our lives more closely parallel the lives of those who lived in the years 1490 to 1550. In those years, there were dramatic transformations that in many ways are reminiscent of our times. As Columbus went to America, we are going into space and below the sea. As in the Reformation, spirituality is being transformed as we are finding ways to combine the best of Eastern and Western religions. At the end of that sixty-year period, an entirely new social system was in place in Europe. The Middle Ages were over and the Renaissance was in full swing. Perhaps there will be an equally dramatic shift for us as we cross over into the twenty-first century.

We are left to decide which of these two historical times of change is the better model for what we feel is happening in the world now. We should be keen observers of inner and outer change. Of course, it can be argued that since the soul is eternal, then timing is not that important. Whether a new age comes in twenty years or two hundred does not make that much difference in the cosmic scheme of things. Nevertheless, the building of a new world requires choice and action. *The personal strategy we follow as individuals in making our contribution is largely affected by what we expect,* by the type of changing times in which we believe we live. Reading this book and learning the details of the Cayce millennium prophecies should help you decide what you believe.

What's Ahead in This Book

The rest of this book is about the events that may soon be coming and the options that we have. Those choices include a chance to play a pivotal role in shaping the character of the millennium shift as it unfolds. The Cayce predictions always emphasized the inner spiritual powers available to humanity, and they describe us as full participants (not bystanders or victims) in what the next few decades will bring.

The details of those millennium prophecies form the content of the next three chapters. After that we'll explore additional sources of information about the new millennium, including a scientific perspective on earth changes and a cross-cultural comparison of prophecies. The final chapters will return to the theme of our own creative role in these times of change. It's a message of hope and empowerment that helps us see what a truly rich opportunity it is to live in today's world on the threshold of a new millennium.

Chapter 2

ARE EARTHQUAKES COMING?

*I*t has all happened so quickly, so unexpectedly. It began only three weeks ago, but since then the changes have been so great that the world that we used to know is only a memory. Looking back we should have seen the signs that all this was coming. Just the frequency with which the earth was rumbling should have alerted us.

Two months ago there were strong earthquakes in the Mediterranean Sea area. There were some minor eruptions of Mt. Etna, and then Mt. Pelee, which had been quiet for so long, violently erupted. Yet, who would have expected that those signs were an overture to the cataclysms that have followed?

Three weeks ago, on a sunny October morning, in the middle of rush hour traffic, the land began to shake in California. Not the small tremors that these people had come to expect and live with. Instead it was an earthquake of unprecedented intensity and duration. The loss of life and property was so severe that it will be difficult ever to make a count. Portions of what had been dry land that morning are now permanently submerged under more than fifty feet of ocean water.

But things did not stop with California. In the past three weeks *there have come reports from around the world of severe earth changes. Devastating earthquakes and tidal waves in Japan; tremors of record intensity in Turkey and Armenia. There have even been strong earthquakes in northern Europe, although as yet there has been no loss of life there.*

The nation and the world have not yet begun to deal with the effects of what has already happened. In the months to come those of us who have not been directly affected will quickly come to realize how interconnected the world is. The unavailability of food and industrial goods will soon be painfully noticeable. And everywhere there is the rarely spoken fear—what if all we have seen so far is just the beginning?

This scenario is from the imagination of someone who has read the prophecies of earth changes found in the Edgar Cayce readings. Probably every person who has studied this material has created his or her own story of what it would be like to live in a world whose geography was rapidly and violently changing. For most of us, it is a sobering and anxiety-producing exercise.

In many ways the readings that Cayce gave on earth changes have done more to popularize his name than any other part of his work. There is without doubt a sensational quality to the idea of California going into the sea or a once dormant volcano reawakening with a fury. It's the kind of sensational material that sells magazine articles and books. It often seems a shame that so many people know of Edgar Cayce in terms of his visions of a possible earth catastrophe, rather than for his quiet, humble work of helping individuals with physical healing or finding deeper purpose in life.

Perhaps because of the dramatic quality of these few readings on earth changes, they have been frequently misstated and misinterpreted. Perhaps it's fear that causes a person (even unconsciously) to alter slightly one of Cayce's prophecies. Or perhaps there are those who are so frustrated with the way our world is run that they take pleasure in misrepresenting Cayce's prophecies which suggest widespread destruction. A truly outlandish example of such sensationalism took place in December 1994 when the tabloid newspaper *Weekly World News* ran on its cover a picture of Edgar Cayce and the headline "Secret Predictions of America's Greatest Prophet." It went on to claim that in 1945 Cayce recorded in his personal diary a list of never-before-published prophecies. The only problem with this claim is that Cayce ceased giving readings in 1944 and died on January 3, 1945. The bogus list includes ominous statements, completely disconnected from the authentic Cayce millennium prophecies.

Which Cayce Readings Addressed Earth Changes?

In studying the details of the Cayce millennium prophecies, we should keep in mind that the two dozen psychic readings that produced *specific earth change predictions* are only two-tenths of one percent of all the readings he gave in his forty-three-year career! The other readings—more than fourteen thousand of them—were for people with health problems, individuals looking for greater purpose in life, and those seeking spiritual guidance. Even though the vast majority of the Cayce readings don't directly concern earth changes, most of them do *indirectly*. How can this be?

Many of the people getting these readings were starting to feel the strains and ambiguities of a world of accelerating change. Sometimes their health problems were principally stress-induced. Often their confusion about finding meaningful work was the result of a world already beginning to change dramatically. Frequently their spiritual disorientation was due to the same moral dilemmas and ethical challenges that we experience so acutely today.

The more than ninety-nine percent of Cayce's work that some people have dismissed as irrelevant to the Cayce prophecies is, in fact, a part of the whole picture. It contains his world view, and it provides a backdrop against which we can see and understand the more sensational predictions. To look *exclusively* at those two dozen readings that mention earthquakes, volcanos, and tidal waves would be to *miss* the grander portrait that Cayce has painted about the transition into a new millennium. When we examine the Cayce teachings as a whole, then we discover the great purposefulness that stands behind the earth changes that may be coming.

The Cayce prophecies can help us shape our beliefs about the future. But for them to be most effective in doing this, we've got to look at the *whole* of what he stated about changing times. Too often there have been *pieces* of predictions published or quoted in lectures. These fragments can easily create a distorted picture, sometimes serving to stimulate fear. Probably no other portion of the Edgar Cayce material has been more misquoted and misunderstood than his statements about the land mass changes that might accompany the beginning of a new millennium. As already noted, when compared to the immense volume of readings he gave, these predictions of earthquakes, volcanos and tidal waves are almost insignificant in number. And yet, no other readings have had such an impact on the thinking of people who are familiar with his work.

These particular readings are so easily misunderstood because they are often studied improperly and, to make matters worse, are frequently quoted out of context. Rarely does one see a *chronological* examination of what he said on this topic. In the few instances in which timing has been considered, the prophecies are presented in the order in which we can expect to see them materialize; for example, predictions about the year 1936 before predictions about the years 1958 to 1998. However, what if Cayce gave some of his prophecies about 1936 *after* he gave the ones for 1958 to 1998? If we are really to experience prophecy as an unfolding, dynamic phenomenon, then the best study would be to recreate for ourselves what it would have been like to be with Edgar Cayce between 1926 and 1944 and to hear these predictions being made *and sometimes changing* over the years. That is the approach that we will use in this chapter.

The majority of the Cayce prophecies have not yet proved to be right or wrong. The predictions yet to be fulfilled fall into two primary categories: geophysical earth changes and political/

economic prophecies. This chapter will consider each prediction of geophysical change. The prophecies concerning social change and the destiny of the nations will be addressed in the next chapter, "The New Root Race and a New World Order."

Of course, most of us aren't very knowledgeable about seismology (the scientific investigation of earth changes). In my own research of the Cayce millennium prophecies, I found it very useful to engage a professional geologist to help me understand and interpret Cayce's predictions about cataclysmic changes and to relearn what I had been taught about earth science in high school—material I had since forgotten. The details of what I rediscovered and what I newly learned from the geologist are found in Chapter 5. Those facts will help us comprehend what Cayce may have been seeing clairvoyantly about the planet. But first, let's look at the earth change predictions themselves.

A Chronological Study of the Earth Change Predictions

Our examination of the earth changes readings in the sequence given by Cayce begins with the year 1926. Before this date we find no reference to major geological upheaval. In other words, Cayce had been giving readings for more than twenty years before this topic even came up!

In 1926 a man in his early forties asked Cayce for a series of readings on the topic of long-range weather forecasting. At the end of the second reading (#195–32), Cayce offered some additional information on weather conditions and the effects they would soon have. He noted that there was a close relationship between these climatic conditions and human affairs. Astrological influences would also play a role. There would be a particular strong sway by Jupiter and Uranus for a six-day period between October 15 and 20. Significant changes could be expected then. These changes would be seen in the minds and the deeds of individuals *and* on a global level. Some of the changes would be constructive; others, destructive.

But Cayce seemed to envision things that were bound to go beyond just this six-day period: In human affairs unusual conditions would arise. They would be felt in religion, politics, and the social dimension of life—especially in regard to morals and values. Then he cited one example: Prohibition (i.e., regarding the sale of alcoholic beverages) would be overturned in America.

In the final part of this prophecy he turns his attention back to the weather and adds certain geological predictions: Several violent wind storms will be seen soon. And there will be two earthquakes, one in southern California and the other in Japan. Tidal waves will follow the Japanese one, with one especially affecting islands to the south of Japan.

This 1926 prediction about Prohibition was fulfilled. The laws banning alcohol had been approved by Congress in 1919. Historians point to a date somewhat after 1926 when a ground swell of public opinion began to move against Prohibition. It was 1933 before the laws were repealed, but Cayce had accurately perceived this coming shift in the moral attitude of Americans.

What do the records show about the accuracy of the rest of these predictions? They're not very supportive. This 1926 prophecy must be viewed as essentially one that failed to materialize—or at least the earth changes portions of it. There was no significant earthquake or tidal wave in Japan on those dates. A moderate quake hit California on October 22, 1926 (two days beyond the predicted dates). However, it was hardly of the magnitude that we might have expected, considering the fact that Cayce had gone out of his way to bring it up. Earthquakes of equal intensity were happening about every two months in California; there were quakes of about the same strength on July 25, 1926, and January 1, 1927.

After the 1926 reading, *six years* pass before we again find someone asking Cayce about earth changes. In 1932 a thirty-year-old man questioned him carefully about the details of what might happen if severe geological changes were to take place. Cayce gave him three separate earth change readings in 1932, spaced about four months apart. Among these readings are some interesting predictions about the order in which events are to take place.

First, Cayce indicated certain signs to watch for which would signal the beginning of the times of great earth change activity. One indicator would be the breaking up of lands in the South Pacific. He states that the changes here could include either sinking *or* rising. This suggests that we should watch either for island areas hit by earthquakes causing permanent inundation *or* for geological shifts that cause South Pacific land areas to rise even higher above sea level.

Another signal event named by Cayce is to take place at a spot almost exactly opposite on the globe, in the Mediterranean Sea, possibly an eruption of Mt. Etna (on the island of Sicily).

When asked when to expect such indicators, Cayce answered that seen from one perspective, these signs had already begun. However, it would likely be 1936 when such changes would be clearly apparent.

Then he was asked whether this would trigger earth changes that would affect North America. His answer was a clear warning of the possibility of severe destruction. All over the country there might come minor and major shifts. But directly targeted was the North Atlantic seaboard, with New York and Connecticut specifically named.

The man who received these readings apparently had a strong personal interest in the fate of Alabama because he asked directly about this area. Cayce predicted that there would be changes there, affecting the northwestern and the extreme southwestern parts of the state, but not until after the ones he had previously described. The timetable he suggested was between 1936 and 1938; however, he made it clear that the changes would be gradual rather than sudden.

Finally, the questioner asked about Norfolk, Virginia, and its vicinity (Cayce's own home area). The prophecy was that changes would come to this area, too, but those were much farther away—

some twenty years after the ones he foresaw for the North Atlantic seaboard and for Alabama.

We're left to wonder how we should take this set of predictions. Obviously, nothing of the scope he mentioned here in 1932 took place in the period from 1936 to 1938. Has the timing simply been delayed? Does the warning sign related to the South Pacific and Mt. Etna still hold? Most scholars of the Cayce material take the position that Cayce was able to see specific, interconnecting conditions beneath the earth's surface; and even if the timing was wrong, the same series of warning events is still relevant.

In the next important series of predictions, Cayce became even more specific. These readings, from early 1933 through 1936, were given to a man in his late forties who lived in San Francisco. There is a strong sense of the unfolding, dynamic quality of prophecy in these passages. The predictions start to change as the months go by and Cayce is asked repeatedly about the fate of San Francisco.

Cayce began in February 1933 sounding quite sure that in 1936 there would be a major destruction of San Francisco. He couldn't have been more blunt. When asked to compare this coming quake to the famous one in 1906, he said, "This'll be a baby beside what it'll be in '36!" (#270–30).

By mid-1934 he was less inclined to specify dates. The same questioner had come back and wanted more details about 1936 (#270–32). He wondered if the predicted earth changes were so fixed and predetermined that Cayce could clairvoyantly describe the Pacific coastline of America after the earthquakes. Now Cayce seemed to back away from any specific chronology, while still affirming that earthquakes in this area were *due* and that it was written in the cosmic scheme of things that they would happen *at some point*.

But even more significant, Cayce stated that what was to transpire depended upon the attitudes of individuals and groups— something so important to Cayce's prophecies about changing times that we'll look at it much more closely in Chapters 7 and 8. Of course, this is a radical idea that has no place in mainstream geology.

The notion that human psychology or daily behavior (short of rash acts such as detonating underground nuclear explosions) could affect earthquakes seems like nonsense to the typical earth scientist.

By June 1936, he had *backed away* from his San Francisco prediction for that year, stating that he no longer saw any great material damage coming to that city for the coming year. However, he went on to predict that there would be some major earthquake activity in areas to the east and to the south of San Francisco, places where there had not been previous damage.

He then went on to give more details about the factors that affect earthquakes. In addition to the obvious geological ingredients (internal movements of the earth) and to the more esoteric influence of people's thoughts and deeds, he added something else: astrological influences. He asserted that earth changes are impelled at least partially by planets and stars in relationship to the earth.

Next came one of his most famous prophecies concerning the West Coast of America, of a warning sign for which people could be alert. Significant eruptions at one of two volcanos would be the sign—either Mt. Vesuvius on the island of Sicily or Mt. Pelee on the island of Martinique in the West Indies. If either were to take place, then *within three months* severe flooding would be widespread as a result of major earthquakes. The areas specifically mentioned were the southern coast of California plus the areas between Salt Lake and the southern portions of Nevada.

Much has been made of this prediction in the decades since it was given. Stretching the truth of the matter, some people have claimed that Cayce predicted California "falling into the ocean." Various coastline maps purported to be based on the Cayce predictions show the vast amounts of North America gone, with the Pacific coming in to Utah or even farther east.

What's more, there has been considerable misunderstanding about the warning. The reading clearly predicts that the major flooding would occur *within* three months of the eruption. It does not say, as many have misquoted, that once Mt. Vesuvius or Mt.

Pelee erupts in a major way, then California residents have a three-month safety or grace period in which to sell their houses and get out!

Finally, the series of earth change predictions from June 1936, concludes with this prophecy: there will be greater seismic upheavals in the Southern Hemisphere than in the Northern. Earlier predictions indicated that the earth changes would be a *worldwide* phenomenon—not just something confined to America. Because many more specific references to catastrophic changes point to America than to other countries, some people have mistakenly believed that Cayce predicted America would be hardest hit. Others have gone so far as to believe that Cayce implicitly suggested that America is especially deserving of punishment. However, this unambiguous prophecy about the Southern Hemisphere puts that mistaken notion to rest. In fact, there is a more plausible and very simple reason that the majority of Cayce's predictions concerned changes occurring in America. The people receiving the readings were most often Americans and were naturally more inclined to *ask* about their own part of the world. People from Alabama worried about what would happen to Alabama; people from San Francisco, about that city. Cayce generally met people at the level of their own concerns, so naturally we have a majority of predictions about earthquakes and flooding in America. But this frequency shouldn't give us a distorted view of his vision of the global scope of these changes.

In fact, the most international of the prophecies was given in 1934—in one of the so-called world affairs readings. These were readings given about political, economic and sociological factors for the world as a whole. Some of Cayce's most important prophecies are found in this series—both prophecies about earthquakes *and* predictions about changing human affairs.

In January 1934, Cayce gave the fifteenth reading in this series (#3976–15). Here he made it clear that the coming earth changes would be spread throughout the world. In fact, this set of earth change prophecies has become the most often quoted portion among all his predictions. In this set of visionary statements he was clearly speaking about a forty-year time span between 1958 and 1998 as marking the *beginning* of the changes he listed. This point has often been missed in articles and books about Cayce's prophecies. The readings do *not* say that all of the changes will be accomplished by 1998, rather that the forty years ending in 1998 encompass the beginning of major global upheavals. *We might well expect them to continue into the twenty-first century.* Here are the specific predictions for world changes prophesied to *commence* in the forty years between 1958 and 1998:

1. There will be a breaking up of the land mass of the western portion of America.

2. The larger part of Japan will go into the sea.

3. There will be certain changes to the northern parts of Europe that will happen so quickly that it might be called "in the twinkling of an eye."

4. Lands will rise up out of the Atlantic Ocean off the east coast of America.

5. Major upheavals will hit the Arctic and Antarctica.

6. Volcanos will erupt, especially in the tropics.

7. A shifting of the poles will alter climatic conditions. For example, certain frigid and semitropical areas will become tropical.

In that same reading he was asked more specifically to make predictions for world changes that very year—1934. Although he clearly missed the mark with many of the statements, many scholars of Cayce's work agree with parapsychologists who point out that precognition (or prophecy) is the most difficult form of psychic ability. Predictions require the seer to operate in a dimension of consciousness that is beyond the normal constraints of time and space, but then to articulate his visions in terms of a specific time frame. We'll address in Chapter 8 some of the factors that may have come into play when Cayce's millennium prophecies failed to materialize by the date he stated. For now, let's consider these prophecies from reading 5749–15, even though they may not have happened when Cayce said they were most likely to take place.

1. Open waters will appear in the northern portion of Greenland, presumably another effect of climatic alterations.
2. The new lands arising from the Atlantic will more specifically be located in the Caribbean Sea area.
3. South America will be "shaken from the uppermost portion to the end."
4. In the Antarctic region, new land will arise off Tierra del Fuego.

Several of these earth change predictions seem to relate directly to Cayce's vision of a pole shift. This is a frightening notion if it's taken at face value. The destruction that might come from a shift in the rotational axis of the earth would be immense. Of course, some interpreters of the Cayce millennium prophecies have suggested that his visions were in this case symbolic or metaphorical references to worldwide humanity getting a new orientation or set of values. But the fact remains that the pole shift prophecy, given more than once by Cayce, is stated as a literal event to come. And in one prophetic reading he offers a specific time frame. When asked what changes would happen in 2000 or 2001, he answered, ". . . there is a shifting of the pole. Or a new cycle begins" (#826–8).

Two final readings in our chronological sequence are especially significant. Both were given in the later years of Cayce's work. The first, given in 1939, was mentioned in Chapter 1. A woman who had studied the three-hundred-year-old prophecies of Jacob Boehme asked Cayce to comment on what was coming. Cayce's prophetic reading for her contains important statements concerning the intensity of the millennium changes:

1. In 1998 we will find a great deal of activity that has been created by the gradual changes that are coming about.
2. As to the changes, the change between the Piscean and the Aquarian Age is a gradual, not a cataclysmic one.

So this gives a somewhat different angle on the future than some of the other Cayce millennium prophecies may have implied. This set of predictions—among the last ones given by Cayce—minimize the likelihood of a cataclysmic future. Instead, these millennium prophecies, offered in 1939, present the image of an earth that will undergo *gradual* alterations. Rather than an apocalyptic transition from the so-called Piscean age to an Aquarian era, possibilities exist for a more piecemeal change, even though that gradual scenario still includes dramatic events. (An apparent discrepancy exists between some cataclysmic prophecies and other predictions that sound more gradual. The topic will be addressed more fully in Chapter 5.)

The final important earth change predictions came in 1941 to a woman in her mid-sixties. Very detailed descriptions were offered of the future map of American (#1152–11). Here again, Cayce's timing seems to be off, because phrases such as "in the next few years" suggest that at least some of these changes would have happened by now. However, the enumeration of those changes was *preceded* by the words "changes here are gradually coming about," which suggests that these events may take a while to unfold. In summary, here is what Cayce presented in his final millennium prophecy reading about earth changes:

1. Geographic alterations are coming for most of America. They will be experienced especially along the two coasts, but also in the central part of America.

2. New land will appear up out of the Atlantic and the Pacific. Other coastal areas that are currently dry land will become "the bed of the ocean."

3. These inundations won't be limited to America. Some of the battlefields of World War II (going on as this reading was given) will eventually be submerged places.

4. Affected portions of the East Coast will include the New York City area. However, this will not happen as soon as many of these other changes, and will rather be in some other generation.

5. Much sooner than the changes along the northern Atlantic

seacoast will be alterations along the south Atlantic. Portions of the Carolinas and Georgia will become permanently submerged.

6. The drainage basin for north central America will be altered so that waters from the Great Lakes will empty into the Mississippi River basin (and into the Gulf of Mexico) rather than via the St. Lawrence River.

7. Severe changes for Los Angeles and San Francisco will happen well before any changes coming for New York.

8. Certain "safety lands" exist—places less vulnerable to the coming changes. Among these safety lands of North America are southeastern Virginia (e.g., Virginia Beach, where Cayce's own readings had instructed him to move in the early 1920s for reasons more complex than just potential earth changes), portions of Ohio, Indiana, and Illinois, much of the southern and the eastern portions of Canada.

The notion of "safety lands" is a provocative one. It easily captures our imagination because it's natural to want a place of refuge when such global threat is predicted. However, we need to be very careful as we interpret this millennium prophecy from Cayce. He does *not* say that these are the only places that will be safe.

But what if we could somehow identify all the locations that would be on such a list of "places to be spared." Does that mean that we should all try to move to such a spot? Maybe that's not what Cayce meant. First, let's realize just how inconceivable it really is that *any area* of America (or any country, for that matter) would be unaffected if the predicted earth changes do occur. Even if that effect isn't geological, it will surely be felt in terms of food, energy, or most importantly, the emotional ties we have with other people.

Most bluntly put: there is *no* place to go and sit out the changes. Thinking for just a moment about America, this nation has grown to the point where we are one interdependent people. The very resources with which we live our lives have come to us through a complex exchange involving countless other people. If one aspect of the whole is interrupted—by an earthquake or any other catastrophe—it will be felt throughout our nation and beyond. Just imagine, for example, the impact on our food supplies if there are huge earthquakes in California.

And this same principle governs the world, as well. We are a world community. Isolationism is no longer an option for any country. When something occurs that disturbs the balance, then it's usually felt within days throughout the world.

What does this principle of interrelationship tell us about so-called "safety lands"? For one thing, it makes us look very carefully at our definition of the word "safety." What could Cayce have really meant? On the one hand, he may have been trying to identify actual areas of the continent where there would be little or no flooding or shaking. And yet how could any spot be entirely "safe"? Cayce's own oceanfront hometown of Virginia Beach seems particularly vulnerable, even though it was mentioned several times as a safe place. If the prophecies prove to be correct—if, for example, land rises off the east coast of America—logic suggests that these upheavals would at least cause *some* coastal flooding. It's already happened with sub-hurricane level "nor'easter" storms. Earthquakes and land formation in the Atlantic would almost certainly cause destructive flooding.

All this suggests that we need to look for other meanings to the phrase "safety lands." *To assert that there is any **private** safety would be inconsistent with Cayce's total philosophy about the millennium.* Authentic safety must fundamentally rest upon being secure spiritually. No soul is "safe" just because it's outside the path of material harm. Real security is an inner state. We are safe when we are right with God and when we are in alignment with the ideals that we've set. For example, in 1942 one person asked if he would be safe in his hometown of New York—that is, safe from bombing or enemy attack. Cayce's answer points to the deeper meaning of safety and security: "Why should he not? If he lives right!" (#257–239).

A new theory is needed for the concept of "safety lands" as we move into the new millennium. It need not contradict the literal interpretation of these words, but it should be complementary and demonstrate how the notion of safety may have multiple levels of meaning.

Here's one possibility: Cities, regions, and even entire states can create by the attitudes and actions of its people a kind of group consciousness. And that collective mind and energy gives a location a particular vibration. In turn, that vibration—if it's resonant to spiritual values—can afford its people a sort of protection. This protection *might* be from outside threats or even disturbances of the earth. But more importantly, in times of upheaval or severe testing, it affords a protection for the individual *from those parts of the self that would lead to fear and doubt.* That's the real threat—that we might lose faith in ourselves, our future, and our Creator.

Cayce's readings speak in detail about such a concept of vibration for a particular location: "Each state, country, or town makes its own vibrations by or through the activities of those that comprise same" (#262–66). Although it's hard to describe logically, this is something that most of us have intuitively felt. When we visit a new location, we can often sense or feel something intangible about that place. We can perceive its collective spirit. We might verbalize such an impression with words like, "I just really feel at home here!" or, when the vibration doesn't match our own, "I need to get out of here because something about this place keeps me from being myself."

And so, what does all this suggest about Cayce's prophetic statement in 1941? What about that rather limited list of areas that would be safe from earth changes in North America? Perhaps he was identifying those areas of the country that had especially large numbers of people who were creating a vibration or aura of attunement. However, that was 1941. It's reasonable to hope and expect that since that time many more locales in America (and throughout the world) have developed to the status of "safety lands." Even though in the future some of these places may be shaken physically—even though every one of them will feel the effects in *some* way if the earth changes do take place—they may,

nevertheless, be places of special opportunity. These special locations may help people stay psychologically and spiritually safe in
times of change, because of the way in which in the collective
consciousness there brings out the best in individuals in times of
crisis.

We don't have to move to one of the existing "safe" locations.
We can each work to build that status for the community in which
we already live.

Chapter 3

THE NEW ROOT RACE AND A NEW WORLD ORDER

The first century of the new millennium will see a whole new way of living on earth—a change even more drastic than the one five hundred years ago when the Middle Ages ended and the Renaissance began. A new consciousness in humanity will arise in the twenty-first century—something that is so completely different that Cayce called it a "new root race." It will profoundly affect political, social, economic, and scientific aspects of our society.

The expression "root race" is found in several metaphysical systems of thought, and it is *not* a reference to racial differences as we typically think of them. Instead, it refers to a new order of human being. The Cayce millennium prophecies challenge us to imagine that we are on the verge of a dramatic new beginning, a new root race. One critical aspect of the consciousness of this new root race concerns an understanding of material versus nonmaterial life. In the new millennium we can expect a revolutionary change: the universal acceptance of the fact that we survive physical death. The continuity of life will be accepted, not just as a statement of religious faith, but as a mainstream scientific reality.

Of course, the early signs of this widespread understanding are all around us, led by research into out-of-body experiences and near-death experiences. These findings are dramatic—some would say nearly incontrovertible—for anyone who looks objectively at the research data. Truly we live in times when a remarkable convergence is taking place on this age-old question of survival. Religion and science are coming to the same conclusion.

Nevertheless, strong cultural forces work against this new agreement. Certain elements of our society would just as soon we dismiss or forget such an important fact as our own timeless existence as spiritual beings. Much of our impatient, consumer-driven culture depends on the emotions of fear and desire—the very feelings that so easily melt away when we accept the continuity of life. And so, there is still considerable work to be done if the consciousness of a new root race is really to take hold and guide the world.

How might this Cayce prediction about overcoming the fear of death actually unfold? The development of a certain form of psychic perception may play a great role in such a change of consciousness. (We'll look more broadly at the topic of psychic awareness later in this chapter.) If large numbers of the human family evolve clairvoyant abilities, imagine what might be the result. Perhaps people would begin to "see" and communicate with those who have passed on. Using the same type of expanded sight that allows someone to see auras, people in the new millennium might perceive the spiritual world bodies of friends and loved ones.

Such a development would have tremendous impact on the values and awareness of humanity. So much of human behavior has long been motivated by a fear of death, by uncertainty about our long-term future as individual beings. Competition and aggression stem largely from the drive to survive and strengthen our sense of power and permanence. If it was a common *experience* to know that death is merely a transition to a new way of living, we can guess that efforts for peace and cooperation in the world would be enhanced.

This speculation dovetails nicely with a biblical prophecy about times of change. Certain verses from the Bible seem to predict that the reappearance of the Christ is to be associated with a period in which the dead will be resurrected. But how probable is it, we might wonder, that corpses will crawl out of the graves? Another interpretation is that *experientially* it will be *as if* the dead have been resurrected. In other words, to those of us still alive in flesh bodies, it will be as if the dead have come back to life—because we will sense them and communicate with them in their astral or etheric forms. Perhaps the biblical prophecy means that the reappearance of Christ will come at a time in history when humanity has developed its spiritual sensitivity to the point where other dimensions of life can be readily sensed and experienced.

Humanity has flirted with this breakthrough principle in the past, according to Cayce. The new root race will possess an awareness similar in many ways to one that was present on the earth long ago. In ancient times, he said, there were societies based on an understanding of the inherent oneness of all energy and the continuity of soul-life. The opportunities for humanity in the twenty-first century and beyond are *not* merely a return to something we had many millennia ago; but, one task of the new root race is to go back and reclaim certain elements of the human legacy that have been ignored or forgotten.

The trigger for this collective recall is to be an astounding archaeological discovery. According to the Cayce millennium prophecies, this event is a strong possibility for the years right at the turn of the twenty-first century. In several places on the globe, records can be found of an extraordinary human civilization which predates by many thousands of years the earliest known advanced civilization. That culture had developed many sophisticated scientific ideas, including the harnessing of solar energy via specialized crystals, plus advanced energy medicine techniques. What's more, that civilization possessed a knowledge base that connected their religious understanding with their scientific principles, just as we are on the verge of doing at the start of our own new millennium.

If the traces of such a civilization—victim of its own mistakes, internal discord about purpose, and ultimate self-destruction—

could be found now, it might be one of the most important breakthroughs in recent history. The Cayce millennium prophecies suggest it could be just around the corner. Those records are to be
found in any of three spots:

1. Beneath the sands in front of the Sphinx. A small, pyramidlike
Hall of Records is buried there, according to Cayce, and just waiting
to be unearthed. Among the three possibilities, this is the location
about which Cayce was most specific; he saw an underground passageway coming from the paw of the Sphinx that would lead archae-
ologists to the tremendous find. In recent years, research teams
have been actively investigating Cayce's hypothesis. They have
used noninvasive technologies such as underground mapping radar
to discover intriguing anomalies (e.g., unexpected spaces or cav-
ernlike areas) for which the Egyptian government may eventually
permit limited drilling or excavation.

2. Somewhere on the Yucatan peninsula. Here Cayce was not
as specific, but he suggests that remnants of that same ancient
civilization left records nearly identical to the ones buried in the
other two spots. The best clue about exact location indicates that
the archaeological find could come from investigating an area near
or beneath an existent, ancient temple: "where the temple there
is overshadowing same" (#2012–1).

3. Somewhere near the island of Bimini in the Bahamas. The
Cayce prophecies offer some tantalizing clues about exact underwa-
ter spots to investigate, and limited investigations for the legendary
Atlantis have been going on for several years to test Cayce's theory.

What might be the impact if one or more of these areas yield
evidence of an advanced civilization that was based on sophisticated
understanding of the oneness of all energy and the direct experience
by its people of the soul's survival? Skeptics might argue that it
would have little or no influence on a modern world whose attention
span for news gets shorter every year, whose inhabitants aren't
even interested in history.

But a counterargument can be made that if such an archaeological find coincides with times of turmoil and stress (perhaps even daunting earth change events), it could well trigger a whole new way for modern society to see itself. Consider what might happen if we stretch our sense of roots back thousands of years earlier and realize that some of the fruits of civilization we're most proud of were actually accomplished long ago. It might humble us. It might awaken us to the possibility that our own culture is fragile and that in our vulnerability we could suffer a similar fate and practically vanish.

With these background ideas in mind about a new root race—a new kind of humanity for this planet—let's consider some further prophecies and visions of Cayce. Each prophecy is a piece of a grand mosaic. That big picture is ultimately a hopeful and exciting one about the new kind of awareness that is about to emerge. The prophecies of change documented in the remainder of this chapter will cover four areas:

1. international politics and the destiny of nations;
2. a transformation of medical science;
3. expanded human mental capacities, especially via intuition;
4. a new philosophy of material resources and the Law of Supply.

Through these prophecies Cayce tried to help us catch a picture of what it might be like to *live* in the world that stretches into the new millennium, what it might be like as members of this new root race.

The World Affairs Prophecies

Cayce made many surprising, bold statements about the nations of the earth and their destinies. The so-called "world affairs readings" most often focused on questions of Cayce's own day: the Depression and the tensions that eventually led to World War II. However, occasional prophecies looked beyond the war and predicted the course nations would take well into the twenty-first century.

The essential ingredient in these predictions is the need Cayce saw for a "leveling" in the world. In calling for equality he was not associating himself with any particular political system. Rather, his political philosophy, as well as his vision of the direction in which the world must head, focused on *the oneness of humanity.* That "leveling," as the readings called it, is a process that pertains to judgment as well as resources. All persons must be seen as equals in the way they are measured or judged. And all persons must have an equal opportunity to share in the resources that sustain life. This means not only food, shelter, clothing and energy, but also knowledge, appreciation and love, which sustain the mind and soul.

A single reading (#3976–18) given just fourteen months before the outbreak of World War II in Europe best outlines Cayce's visionary ideas about a world in flux: A new order of conditions is eventually to emerge. It will be accompanied by a cleansing at all strata of the society, from the richest to the poorest. Central to the transition will be the principle that each soul is its brother's and sister's keeper. In many elements of society—political, economic, and social—the understanding will emerge that a "leveling" is required.

But Cayce's prophecy goes on to say that these changes won't happen instantaneously or magically. Individuals, groups, and organizations that espouse this ideal of oneness and equality will need to work hard, to practice and apply what they believe in. The transition may not be easy because it will require a new way of thinking and behaving in society: "There cannot be one measuring stick for the laborer in the field and the man behind the counter, and another for the man behind the money changers. All are equal— not only under the material law, but under the spiritual."

The prophecy continues with a warning of great stresses ahead. Family members will find themselves on opposing sides in this struggle. Groups will clash, as will races. But this transition is a part of human destiny. "The leveling must come." Our only real protection comes from a single source, according to the way this prophecy ends: by personally setting a high spiritual ideal and then diligently living it in relationship to the people around us.

In one passage the readings made clear that this task of leveling was not a call for communism, even in the pure sense of the word, thus stated, "Not that all would be had in common as in the communistic idea, save as to keep that balance, to keep that oneness" (#3976–19). On the other hand, the Cayce millennium prophecies spoke even more strongly against the notion of survival of the fittest (or of the greatest and most powerful), which has characterized pure capitalism. It will not do for us to sit back and say that those people who are exploited are simply not motivated enough. Nor will it do to slip into a *distorted* notion of reincarnation and soul-level responsibility, claiming that the disadvantaged of the world are merely meeting their own karma. Cayce's visionary image of international affairs was that peace can come only when the ideal of "I am my brother's and sister's keeper" has been adopted.

How will that come about? What changes will we have to see in specific nations if that purpose and ideal is ever to be achieved? The analysis given by Cayce was that the problem lies in a particular tendency of all nations to "set some standard of some activity of man as its idea" (#3976–29). In other words, nations have different concepts about:

1. how human life should be evaluated,
2. what constitutes the good life,
3. what constitutes justice, and
4. what scope of authority a government should have over individuals.

And the efforts of nations to impose their own standards on other nations create international tensions and wars. For each major nation Cayce saw a work or a change to be done.

In the case of Russia, Cayce foresaw a tremendous transition. He warned that there would never be peace in that country until there was freedom of speech. He predicted a reawakened religious spirit in Russia, which if developed would be the hope of the world. He also clearly predicted a major role in world leadership for Russia.

When asked to comment in 1938 about the prospects for Russia, he predicted that a new understanding would come to a troubled people. Oppression and self-indulgence had produced the excesses of communism, and until there was authentic freedom—of speech and worship—turmoil would persist.

The theme of religious freedom had actually been part of a Cayce prophecy six years earlier in reading #3976–10. In his vision of the world of a new millennium, Cayce saw Russia's religious develop- ment as pivotal. He said, "On Russia's religious development will come the greater hope of the world." These words indicate that spiritual transformations among Russians will trigger changes in people and nations worldwide. What's more, we can expect that religious progress in Russia will so ease international tension that it will make room for hopeful, new conditions to arise.

Years later, in 1944, yet another Cayce prophecy used the theme of hope in relation to the Russians. The key to Russia fulfilling its potential will be freedom and the ideal of service ("that each man will live for his fellow man").

What sort of timing can we expect for such planetary leadership, and in what form? The Cayce millennium prophecies made clear that such a potential can be fulfilled only by Russia joining in cooperative efforts with the United States. As to timing, he stated that "the principle has been born" (#3976–29). What could he have meant by this? In 1944, when this reading was given, a group of souls had recently incarnated into Russia with a purpose to turn that nation around—to make it a champion for peace and permit a religious rebirth within its borders. It took years for this possibil- ity to crystallize. Those souls born in 1940 or thereabouts were unable to assume positions to exert much influence on the decision-making process of the government until they were at least fifty years old. Throughout the Cold War era that nation was characterized by aged leadership. The timing seems about right that in 1989 extraordinary changes began to take place in Russia. Certainly the Gorbachev-led changes were just a beginning, a start toward what Cayce predicted. But the transformation is about more than just one man's political efforts. The group of souls that Cayce envisioned still has considerable work left to do. They must remember the purpose for which they came and not get caught up in the ways of the old system.

What about prophecies concerning the United States? In the case of America, Cayce had some strong words of warning, but words of promise as well. Again the principle of leveling came up. There is a warning that unless creative, loving steps are taken to insure greater equality within this nation, there will come a revolution, a physical, armed struggle, because this is the means that some people will resort to when they feel helpless to effect change in any other way. Cayce did not give an endorsement of such methods—only a warning that they may be just ahead for us.

The prophecies regarding America emphasize freedom and the leadership role that America is to play on the world stage—leadership both with responsible expressions of freedom and the deepening of spirituality. Although America is destined to have the opportunity for spiritual leadership as we move into the new millennium, it is by no means certain that we will collectively claim that special role. The outcome rests with our use of the freedoms we possess.

The ideal of freedom is one to be admired, but Cayce questioned just how honestly America lives that ideal. In a prophecy given in 1944—some two decades before the civil rights movement—he observed that our nation was being run in such a fashion that the hearts and minds of many people were "bound." This surely refers in large part to minorities, such as the African-American citizens of the country. He identified three aspects of life where this constriction affected many people: speech, worship, and the basic physical needs of life. It could be persuasively argued that progress has been made in the fifty years since that warning, but no doubt we still have considerable room for improvement.

Another prophetic reading identified the great fear of Americans: servitude in any form. We are afraid of losing our freedom, and yet we may have distorted what that very word means. We have made the quality of obedience a sign of weakness and in so doing have undermined our spirituality. *Our actions cannot fulfill the challenge and opportunity of spiritual leadership in the world if we have a self-serving definition of freedom.* True freedom comes from the desire and ability to be obedient—not to another nation but to God. And in our obedience to God we will be called to loving, responsible service. This means national actions that place a high priority on the well-being of others. Although it seems paradoxical, Cayce states that the nation that would be greatest—and most free—must be a servant to all.

Cayce clearly articulated this principle as the guiding definition for national greatness in the twenty-first century. It's a hard principle for our nation, or for any nation, to understand and to live. Misunderstanding it, we slip into what Cayce called the great sin of America: pride. This quality could stand between America and its spiritual destiny to provide leadership for the world. *Pride, not just on the part of the government, but in the people as individuals, needs to be overcome.* Our tendency to boast separates us from other nations and people of this world; it puts up barriers between Americans and the citizens of other countries.

Once Cayce was asked very directly about America's spiritual destiny. He answered that every nation has a specific spiritual destiny—that each one is led by forces from the heavens. America can fulfill her destiny only by adopting greater brotherhood and love of others. Otherwise the leadership of the world will once again move westward: "... Each and every nation, is led—even as in heaven. If there is not the acceptance in America of the closer brotherhood of man, the love of the neighbor as self, civilization must wend its way westward ..." (#3976–15). From other Cayce prophecies we can ascertain that that westward movement would be to eastern Asia.

The key to whether or not leadership eventually moves is this question: What will individuals *do with* the spiritual knowledge they have? It is not so much the choices of government officials or the legislative bills passed by Congress that determine whether or not we will fulfill our national challenge. Instead, it's what each of us does as an *individual* that will collectively create our future.

Perhaps the beneficiary of a movement of civilization westward would be China. This mysterious nation has only in the past few years made efforts to become part of the world community once again. Its resources and people are vast. Its spiritual legacy from several thousand years is matched by no other major nation except India. It is exciting to imagine what good could be done by these people if their national ideal and purpose became unity and spirituality. It was just such a vision that Cayce put forth in the world affairs prophecies. China will eventually be the "cradle of Christianity, as applied in the lives of men" (#3976–29). However, no time frame accompanies this prediction beyond the caution that "it is far off as man counts time."

Are we then to expect that someday there will be widespread Christianity in the world's most populous nation? A few decades ago that seemed nearly impossible. During the 1960s what churches there were had to be closed and religious activity was forbidden. But now there are signs of change, and maybe Cayce's prophecy will yet come true. Recent newspaper accounts tell an amazing story. The World Council of Churches reports that Christianity is growing in China "at breathtaking speed." A council delegation returned from an eleven-day trip to China in the spring of 1996 and made a "conservative estimate" of baptized Christians: ten million and growing fast.

But maybe the proliferation of Christian churches isn't exactly what the Cayce prophecy meant. The key word in the prediction is Christianity as *applied* in human lives. Perhaps it is in this country that *the way of living with each other* that Jesus proposed will find a willing climate. Whether or not the Chinese accept Jesus is secondary to this prophecy. Here is a people, in Cayce's estimation, who may be especially ripe for the application of Christ's teachings. In doing so, they would surely assume the spiritual leadership of civilization on this planet. But, as the prophecy says, this may be many years away. We have our own work to do closer to home right now, toward that same ideal.

Finally, it should be noted that amongst all the world affairs predictions of revolution, turmoil, changes of government and so forth, there is still a message of profound *encouragement.* It is so easy for us to be discouraged by current events and to dwell upon the great confusion among nations. However, Cayce may have been able to look at the world from a broader perspective. In that remarkable state from which he gave his prophetic readings, he may have been able to see the unfolding of history in terms of ages and not just the decades and centuries we see. And from this vantage point, he said that *there is hope.* For our own times, near the turn of the millennium, Cayce foresaw a tremendous seeking in our world. Remarkable numbers of people would desire oneness with God and an understanding of God's purposes. The seeking would be greater than it had been for ages! And it will continue to increase each year, giving us good reason to be hopeful.

Prophecies of Health and Healing in the Twenty-first Century

Cayce made many hopeful predictions about healing in the new millennium. In fact, there is considerable evidence of his skill at predicting trends in medical science. For example, in 1927 he boldly asserted that the day would come when a person's overall physical condition could be completely diagnosed from a single drop of blood. At that time it seemed fanciful, but the day is fast approaching when medical technology can do exactly that.

His prophetic statements about finding a remedy to cancer are also noteworthy. In the 1920s and 1930s, Cayce spoke on repeated occasions of a different orientation to the prevention and cure of many (if not all) cancers, one of strengthening the immune system. This ran counter to the prevailing wisdom about cancer in Cayce's own era. It wasn't until the early 1960s that a failure in the immune system was even seriously considered by mainstream medicine as linked to some cancers.

In a few of his psychic readings on cancer, Cayce spoke of culturing the blood—that is, removing a small portion, mixing it with prescribed solutions, and then reinfusing this cultured blood, apparently to stimulate the white blood cells. This procedure, although never carried out for any of the cancer patients Cayce diagnosed, closely resembles an experimental method of modern cancer research. In the twenty-first century we may well see that Cayce was far ahead of his time in associating cancer with the immune system.

But such novel techniques are simply fascinating details of a much bigger picture. Cayce envisioned for the new millennium a profoundly different kind of human understanding about how the body stays healthy and how it reestablishes health when something goes wrong. Those prophecies are based on the emergence of a fundamental conception of the human being which is holistic. In fact, Cayce was characterized as the "father of holistic medicine" by an article in the *Journal of the American Medical Association*.

In the twenty-first century, he believed we will begin to appreciate fully that the human being is a set of interpenetrating energy fields—physical, emotional, mental, and spiritual. The concept of psychosomatic illness (already widely accepted as an explanation for certain ailments) will have greatly expanded. Not only will we appreciate the authenticity of psychosomatic *health*, but our approach to healing will also appreciate the deep, spiritual undertones to many illnesses and maladies.

To encapsulate Cayce's vision of medicine in the new millennium, it will be *energy medicine*. Patterns in the flesh, in our emotional outlook, in our attitudes, and in our deepest sense of purpose will all be understood as expressions of energy. Although modern medical science is only begrudgingly beginning to consider the subtle forms of energy that mystics like Cayce describe, the day may be soon ahead when they will be widely recognized.

As noted earlier, Cayce even predicted that in the centuries just ahead humanity will understand that religion and science must merge. A starting point is the discovery that *electricity* is one way for us to understand the creative force that is God. That is to say, electrical forces are the key to the elusive "vital force" healers and metaphysicians have sought for ages.

That is not to say that Cayce advocates giving up our worship of God as the imparter of high ideals and moral principles. Cayce's innovative concept of electricity is *not* an invitation to worship electrical batteries or the products of the electronics industry. Instead, it's a recognition that there is *one fundamental life force*, which is creative and healing in its nature. That divine force expresses itself in the three-dimensional material world as positive and negative charge—i.e., electricity. As one Cayce passage put it: "For materiality is—or matter is—that demonstration and manifestation of the units of positive and negative energy, or electricity, or God" (#412–9).

The potential consequences of such a breakthrough understanding by humanity is astounding. For example, an energy medicine of the twenty-first century will *begin* to show us how new forms of electrical therapy can stimulate healing and even regeneration. Experimentation in the late twentieth century is already beginning to show in some animal studies that electrical impulses can promote the regrowth of limbs. In the new millennium, electricity will be seen as the fundamental building block of everything we experience in material life, including our bodies.

So what might be possible in the decades and centuries to come? One exciting possibility is the sustenance of human life to age 120 or even 150. This is a lifespan that Cayce suggested is within our reach and would even be normal if we began to practice health care appropriately. He even went so far as to say that a human being really ought to be able to regenerate himself and live as long as he desires, *if* he is ready to "pay the price" in terms of the sacrifices and commitments required for a holistically balanced lifestyle.

Several basic features make up Cayce's health care approach, and he predicted they will form the foundation of our health and healing practice in the new millennium. In his book *Keys to Health* which summarizes the essence of Cayce's visionary health philosophy, Eric Mein, M.D., identifies several key points about what is possible for a health science of the future. Each of these points concerns our own attitudes and approaches to health and wellness:

1. An expanded view of the interconnections of the body. Cayce tried to show, well before most medical experts were willing to listen, that tho oyotcms of the body are deeply interlinked. Slowly evidence is mounting of the wisdom of this idea. For example, as the new medical science of psychoneuroimmunology has begun to demonstrate, the mind, the nervous system, and the immune system are all connected. Even though this link might make sense to the layman, it was not until recently that scientific research had any evidence that these three human systems directly affect each other.

2. Self-responsibility. We'll certainly still have physicians in the twenty-first century, but we will come to see health and healing as processes that require our own participation first.

3. No magic bullet. Modern medical research has provided us with so many impressive medications that it's easy to slip into expecting a magic pill for any ailment. But in spite of the wonderful progress in pharmacology, the fact remains that for many (if not most) human maladies it's the body itself that creates the healing, not a magic medicine. Dr. Mein writes that by some estimates as many as seventy-five percent of the patients who visit their doctors have illnesses that will get better on their own, if they are going to get better at all.

In the twenty-first century medicine that Cayce envisions, there will be formulas, pills, and drugs. But we will have learned more about the marvelous self-healing forces that can be elicited from within ourselves. This potential is beautifully illustrated by the way that most current prescription drugs work within our bodies: they mimic what the body has the potential to do for itself. For example, morphine can eliminate pain because the chemical structure of its molecules attach to specific receptors that exist on cell membranes. But morphine molecules can block pain only because human cellular chemistry already provides receptors for certain molecules to do so. That chemical possibility existed in the human body for thousands and thousands of years before poppies were ever refined to make the drug morphine. And, in fact, in the 1970s medical researchers discovered why. The body has a drug of its own—endorphins—that blocks pain naturally. In the medicine of a new millennium we will discover many more ways in which drugs are only a temporary, stopgap measure until the patient can learn for himself how to elicit his body's own healing forces.

The Cayce millennium prophecies include several specific breakthroughs in medical understanding that might be just ahead for us. Each one is related to the innovative holistic philosophy he pioneered, among them these promising areas for discovery:

1. The majority of people in mental hospitals will show measurable improvement from properly administered osteopathic adjustments to the spinal vertebrae.

2. The mysterious skin disorder psoriasis will be completely curable using a specialized diet, specific herbal teas, and osteopathic adjustments.

3. Many cases of asthma will be treated as a disorder of the nerve reflexes, using osteopathic adjustments, along with a specialized diet and improved eliminations.

4. Although slow acting in its healing effect—requiring three to seven years to cure—a new therapy for multiple sclerosis will emerge, one that stimulates the body's ability to absorb the trace mineral gold, plus the use of therapeutic massage along the spine and the extremities.

5. Many who suffer from epilepsy will be significantly helped

by a new form of treatment that recognizes the role played by spinal lesions and a portion of the intestinal tract called the lacteal duct. External castor oil packs on the lower abdomen, along with osteopathic adjustments of particular vertebrae will be key elements of this new therapy.

6. A diet made up of eighty percent alkaline-producing foods (most fruits and vegetables) and twenty percent acid-producing (most meats, grains, and starches) will be identified as the nutritional balance most likely to sustain health. (See Chapter 8 for more details.)

These are just a few of the revolutionary methods Cayce proposes for twenty-first century energy medicine. If even a few of them result in positive findings by medical researchers, they may prove to be among his most important millennium prophecies.

Intuition and Psychic Ability in the Millennium

Another quality of the "new root race" as envisioned by Cayce is psychic sensitivity. In the minds of many people, extrasensory perception and the new millennium seem to go hand in hand. This is probably because psychically gifted individuals have been widely publicized for their descriptions of what may come in the year 2001 and beyond. However, this linkage is not necessarily the proper one. Just because psychics claim to see the future does not mean that most people who live in that future will be psychic themselves. However, Cayce's millennium prophecies about ESP becoming commonplace make sense as a natural outgrowth of something else he predicted: *attunement.* If we imagine a world in which most people are consciously making efforts to align the body and the mind with the spirit, then we have a society ripe for psychic development.

As Cayce put it, psychic experience is *"of the soul."* It is an expression of the spiritual forces manifesting in the material world. When people meditate regularly, watch their dreams carefully and sincerely try to be of service to each other, then the stage is perfectly set for the flowering of clairvoyance, telepathy, and precognition.

However, with the blossoming of these latent abilities come challenges and potential difficulties. One needs only to read the biographies of many modern-day psychics to notice that the development of psychic perception usually creates problems. The predicament in which they found themselves was not due exclusively to the skeptical society in which they lived. These gifted psychics had to wrestle with tough questions that came with being telepathic, clairvoyant or precognitive: For what purposes should such abilities be used? How should intuitive, nonrational sources of information be combined with logical common sense? If coming generations are to be more psychically tuned-in, we might expect that these kinds of questions will be as frequent in one hundred years as are questions today about inflation or global warming.

Cayce's fundamental explanation of how psychic perception works is extremely insightful. It places ESP in a balanced, helpful context. The first principle—as already stated in the phrase "psychic is of the soul"—is that psychic experience can be fully understood only in the framework of a physical, mental *and* spiritual human nature. Add to this a significant second premise: Psychic awareness is a normal and natural response of the mind to the desire to be of service to others. One Cayce reading referred to this orientation as the "love intent," acting as a catalyst upon the unconscious mind. That intention to serve and love opens awareness to the ever-present connection between all souls.

Both of these fundamental principles are rather metaphysical in nature. They depend upon our willingness to think in terms of nonmaterial reality. However, at the same time, Cayce suggested that ESP should be a practical, down-to-earth tool for daily living. It is of little value unless we can find ways to use it productively in materiality—for example, healing baffling diseases (as demonstrated in Cayce's own work) or making insightful leadership decisions that benefit many people. But whatever form it takes, psychic sensitivity needs to be applicable, in a three-dimensional, physical sense.

This brings us to a distinct challenge for how we will respond to awakening psychic abilities within ourselves. What do we do with impressions we receive about others, impressions that we suspect may be accurate extrasensory information? What is the next step if we are praying for someone and unexpectedly get a strong feeling for what that person should do? It is rather disconcerting to imagine that in the new millennium we will have everyone walking around giving unsolicited psychic readings for each other. We must have a balanced way of sharing this information without seeming pushy or invading the privacy of others. If, in fact, psychic experience is to become commonplace in the decades and centuries to come, then it is crucial that we find acceptable approaches for sharing intuitive impressions.

A part of the answer may lie in a willingness to communicate impressions "without forcing the issue," as Cayce put it. In other words, we can relate our inner experiences while simultaneously admitting that they *might not* be telepathic or clairvoyant at all. A dream or meditation experience can be told in such a way that the listener can comfortably refuse to see it as a psychic impression about him or her.

For example, suppose you have a dream in which your next-door neighbor is trying to put out a smoldering fire in his bedroom. You suspect this may be a telepathic dream about his emotional conflicts related to his marriage because several years earlier—during a period when you were having marriage difficulties of your own—you had dreams about trying to put out a bedroom blaze. You now suspect that the dream about your neighbor is telepathic sensitivity to an unspoken problem. Cayce would encourage you to share the dream with him, but in a way that makes it easy for him to respond that your dream must surely be only about yourself. However, in telling the dream the possibility always exists that it may *actually be psychic* in nature and may be received gratefully by your neighbor, allowing him to open up and talk with a sympathetic friend or to admit that he needs a counselor's help.

Related to the same issue is how we treat information that seems to be precognitive in nature. This is tricky, and we can subtly mislead ourselves if we're not careful. What do you do with impressions that appear to be "guidance"? Sometimes that information comes in response to prayers asking for direction in a decision. Other times it may come without your particularly seeking it. In either case, a delicate balance is needed between obedience to the inner reality and plain common sense. God wants you to use your logical, intellectual mind—but *not exclusively* that level of mind. To do so is to become rigid and uninspired. On the other hand, soul growth does not come from blind obedience to every subjective impression that comes into awareness.

In a number of readings, Cayce recommended a specific exercise for developing one's psychic perception in making practical life decisions. We can well imagine that in the twenty-first century a technique such as this one will frequently be employed. Here is a detailed outline of the steps in a decision-making procedure that by helping you learn how to receive intuition from universal awareness can stimulate increased psychic development:

1. *Set your spiritual ideal.* You will find instructions on how to do this in the early portion of Chapter 8. It is a matter of identifying the core value of your life. Cayce usually encouraged people to pick a word (e.g., "peace" or "Buddha" or "God") or a short phrase (e.g., "joyful creativity" or "oneness with Christ") to capture a sense of this aspiration for one's own growth and development.

2. *Pose a question*—one that can be answered yes or no—concerning some decision you must make. In working on this exercise, you may choose a simple question or problem that you are currently facing in life, or you may choose one that is profoundly significant to you. Whatever problem you decide to work on, write it out in the form of a yes or no question describing the decision you face. For example, the question "Should I go back to college?" is much

easier to work with than "What should I do now that I have a lot of free time?" The latter is too open ended and avoids a consciously made choice.

3. *Make a conscious yes-or-no decision* in answer to the question you have just posed. Part of our growth in consciousness as souls involves learning how to make decisions properly—ones that are in accord with divine will. Practicing the act of making a careful decision is important. In making that preliminary, conscious decision, you will want to take into consideration all the information you consciously have access to. Be sure that this provisional decision is one you would be willing to carry out.

4. *Measure the tentative decision by your spiritual ideal.* Ask yourself, "Could I follow through on my decision and still be true to my spiritual ideal?" If the answer is yes, you could be true to your ideal, then go on to Step 5. But if it is no, go back to Step 3 and try the opposite decision. Occasionally a person finds that neither a decision of yes nor one of no will allow him to remain true to his spiritual ideal. In that case, the person is not really ready to make a decision, and he should turn to consistent prayer and a deeper analysis of the question being faced.

5. *Meditate,* not on the question, but *for attunement.* With this step we are beginning a process whereby we seek a confirmation from within ourselves of the provisional decision made in Step 3. This confirmation (or denial) is likely to be accurate only to the degree that we have in meditation attuned ourselves to universal awareness. Do not let yourself be tempted into dwelling on the decision during meditation. Put the question aside and have a period of silent focus upon a statement of your spiritual ideal.

6. At the end of your mediation, *ask the question and listen for a yes-or-no answer from within.* This "listening" sometimes elicits a response from an inner voice; at other times, the answer comes as a hunch or an inner impression. Occasionally a person will get nothing at all during this period. In that case, he will want to extend the "listening period" and pay special attention to his dreams. If this is done, a precognitive dream frequently follows, saying, in effect, "If you follow through on the decision you've made, here

are the likely results." One can then consciously judge whether or not the likely consequences are acceptable. If they are not, a change in the decision is called for.

7. *Measure the guided decision by your spiritual ideal.* After receiving a confirmation or denial, either at the end of meditation or by way of a dream, one should once again check to make sure that the latest understanding of the proper choice does not violate the nature of one's own spiritual ideal.

8. *Act on the guided decision.* No form of psychic or intuitive development has much meaning unless we act upon whatever we receive. Be sure to do this in relation to the specific situation on which you have been working with the previous seven steps.

After going through this exercise you may want to repeat each of the steps, especially if the decision you face is an important one. At the end of the procedure, you might wish to record your question, decision and resulting action, as well as your feelings about this exercise. All of this is exactly the process Cayce envisioned for how we would be making important personal decisions in the new millennium.

A New Consciousness About the Law of Supply

We've already seen that in the world affairs readings Cayce made a number of prophetic statements about the destiny of the nations, including some economic prophecies. Chief among them was the likelihood of an armed revolution unless humanity found a way to "level" the playing field, in regard to all the physical necessities of life. His millennium prophecies also addressed the question of *personal* finances. That is, Cayce envisioned a way that people would one day live in relationship to a universal Law of Supply—or, as he called it, the Law of Abundance.

Many people are convinced primarily because of financial pressures that these really *are* times of change. The challenge comes as a test to make do with less. Unfortunately others who could potentially get by with a more modest way of living won't do it. Instead, their frequent response is to go deeper in debt, borrowing against the future. But when a person has borrowed against the future, oftentimes tomorrow looks more and more like something to be avoided. Hope, expectancy and optimism fade because the future toward which they are headed is ever more debt-ridden.

However we personally experience these times of change in regard to finances, the opportunity of the millennium shift is to rediscover that God *is* the source of *all supply* and that by our own consciousness we create the degree of our access to it. In personal advice given to many individuals who came to Cayce because of economic woes, he said that the financial challenge at hand was an opportunity to understand this link between God, one's own consciousness, and material resources.

Ideally we would live in a world guided by the principle that God is the source of all physical supply. It would be a world whose people were fed, sheltered and cared for medically. The personal and physical needs of every individual would be secure. Such a condition is part of Cayce's vision for our future, but we still have considerable work to do in achieving such a consciousness. Until the day comes when all humanity is prepared to adopt this type of awareness, we can only work as individuals to manifest the law.

To understand Cayce's vision of the Law of Supply and how economic healing works, we must begin with a definition of "supply." Think of it as physical resources for living, which include food, shelter, money or anything else of the material world we need. The Bible, the Edgar Cayce readings and so many other teachings all instruct us that God is the source of all supply. In other words, the physical plane of existence is a creation of the Infinite and is sustained by it. The energy that is in food is a projection into matter of God's creative forces. The mineral kingdom—be it oil, gold or whatever—is a manifestation of divine energies of a higher dimension. Even money itself, which symbolizes a kind of earthly power or influence, is only a lesser-dimensional projection of God's power. This idea of power is reminiscent of Jesus' statement to Pilate that he had no power except that which God had allowed him to have.

Note that we have said, "God is the source of supply," not "God is the distributor of supply"; it is a subtle but highly significant distinction. Many people hear the words of the first phrase but understand them as those in the second phrase. This kind of thinking supposes God to be the dispenser of material goods and money. It suggests that if you are on good terms with God, then He will put material rewards in the pipeline for you. And you do not need to have an anthropomorphic notion of God to think in this fashion. Even if you have a more abstract idea of God such as Universal Mind or Creative Forces or Cosmic Love, this sort of outlook can still control your thinking.

But this is not what is meant by God as the source of supply. *God IS supply.* The energies and consciousness of the Divine are infinite, yet they manifest in the three-dimensional physical world. Those manifestations are everything we think of as the resources for material living. It is in *this* sense that God is the source of all supply; but we do not have to coerce Him into a willingness to give us our share. God is not the boss at work who must be convinced that we deserve a raise.

Instead it is by our own consciousness that we create our access to supply. *We* are the dispensers and distributors of the Infinite Energies as they manifest in materiality. By the patterns of our thinking, feeling and acting, we determine as individuals the amount of physical resources to which we have access and responsibility. That means money, food, energy, shelter, clothing, free time, and much more. Contrary to what many still believe, there is *not* a limited supply which can accommodate only a select few. Certainly there may appear to be current shortages in some specific *forms* of supply. But the resources of physical living are obtainable for every person of planet Earth if our consciousness is properly attuned—as individuals and collectively.

However, sometimes our experience seems to contradict this

fundamental principle. Sometimes it doesn't seem that by our consciousness we create our access to supply. We all know of people who seem to have a highly attuned, loving spirit, and yet they still experience material shortages. Some of us may be good examples of this ourselves. To understand what is going on, we may have to look more deeply than the conscious patterns of thinking. The matter of economic healing and supply is the concern of the *soul* and necessarily involves unconscious levels of the mind, especially memory patterns from the present lifetime and past lifetimes. Simply put: We often must be patient in achieving *economic* healing just as we would with *physical* healing. We might prefer a quick metaphysical trick to make us rich. We might be tempted by simplistic positive thinking that promises instant riches, in the same way we might like a pill to take care of illness instead of having to make deep changes of body, mind and spirit.

Many souls have chosen to meet in this lifetime certain karmic patterns from the past which express themselves as the challenges and tests of privation. Certainly a good first step toward healing those conditions (especially the *inner conditions* of the soul) is a positive conscious outlook, even the expectation of better times. If material levels of supply do not alter instantaneously, it is not because the spiritual principle is wrong. Instead it might be that unconscious distortions of mind and emotion change slowly.

Keeping in mind this need for patience, let us consider some of the ways in which we create our access to supply. God is the source not just of supply, but *abundant* supply. By the way in which we understand and respond to this divine characteristic of abundance, we are creating a key aspect of our consciousness toward material supply. The Bible beautifully illustrates God's intent to express Himself abundantly. The story of the loaves and fishes is an excellent example. Not only did Jesus manifest enough food to feed everyone who was there that day, but there was such an abundance of food that tremendous quantities of leftovers were collected.

Yet what does abundance have to do with painful shortages that we may now be experiencing? By a twist of irony, the spiritual law is that our access to supply today is at least in part created by what we have done with *abundant* conditions in the past. In other words, we may be facing difficult challenges of material shortages to help us grow and change our previous tendencies to misuse abundance.

Observe two circumstances in which we have a problem with supply. One is when there is not enough; and we experience discomfort, pain or frustration. Of course, when there is just exactly enough—when supply perfectly matches need—then none of these problems exist and everything is fine. But a second challenging circumstance exists when there is more than enough. It is an often overlooked difficulty which is created when the amount available exceeds the need. What do we do with what is left over? How do we deal with such abundant conditions? The degree to which we deal responsibly and lovingly with the extra amount may clearly depict our real ideal toward material supply.

To understand how this process may have been working in your life, consider some of the categories of supply and some questions about how abundance might affect each one of them. Some of the most important categories are not ones we immediately think of when we consider material resources, but which are still significant aspects of physical life and the gifts granted by God to a soul in its incarnation.

1. *Money.* What do you do when you have a little extra money? How is it used? What desires is it used to fulfill?

2. *Free time.* What do you do with your extra time in the day? Do you waste it or use it creatively?

3. *Energy.* How responsible are you with energy when you are not paying the utility bill? For example, when you stay in a hotel, where you seem to have all the heat, lighting, and hot water you want at no extra expense, how conservation minded are you?

4. *Food.* How careful and responsible are you in taking only the food you genuinely need—or will even be able to eat—when you visit an "all-you-can-eat" restaurant?

5. *Talent and skill.* What do you do when the job you have to

perform requires of you less talent or skill than you already have? Do you do just the minimum acceptable standard or do you fully use the abundance you have and produce a better-than-expected result?

The answers to these and similar questions will help you get a sense of how you deal with abundance. It may give you a clue as to what kind of consciousness and access to supply you are creating for the future. In observing this process you should realize that effects can be produced *across categories.* In other words, misuse of abundance in one area of life can create the need for lessons of shortage in another category. Fortunately, the principle also works in a more positive way, too: responsible use of abundance in one area of life can produce proper supply in another area.

Cayce envisioned that the last four decades of the twentieth century would be a time of testing to prepare us for the challenges of living in the new millennium. Many of those tests have to do directly with material resources and the Law of Supply. Collectively the American people seem to be experiencing the working of this law as a nation. Americans were blessed with an abundance of natural resources and yet have not been ecologically responsible in stewardship. Current problems such as pollution are, in turn, creating difficulties in maintaining the previous levels of energy, clean water and safe air. The same process can be at work for an individual soul. The waste or misuse of resources may have developed in this lifetime or a past one. In either case, it is a pattern of behavior that runs counter to the evolutionary flow of the soul, and it is the soul itself that chooses and creates shortages to stimulate the learning process.

That learning can be straightforward and efficient if the individual chooses to try a new attitudinal and behavioral approach. Or it can be protracted and painful if the shortage is blamed on others and violently resisted. This is not meant to be a call for passivity in the face of poverty. There *are* social injustices in our world that foster poverty. But for any individual soul the work to change such conditions of shortage must begin with personal responsibility and motivation. It *can* be done and *has* been done by specific individuals; and largely by their courageous efforts and example will the acute material shortages of great segments of humankind be transformed in the millennium. It will not come overnight in the year 2001, nor will it arrive magically. But Cayce's visions of the future were hopeful and state that we will some day understand and live purposefully with the Law of Abundance.

A Conclusion About the Cayce Millennium Prophecies

Throughout this chapter and the previous one, we've examined Cayce's visionary statements about the future. Some sound rather frightening, while others quickly inspire hope and enthusiasm for the future. But how are we to understand these predictions about earth changes, geopolitical shifts, and an emerging new life-style? How do we cope with the measure of uncertainty and anxiety they are likely to instill in almost anyone who hears these prophecies? The best answer probably lies in a careful look at the one central theme of the prophecies.

The very *essence* of Cayce's prophecies was not earthquakes or tidal waves or volcanic eruptions—not cities destroyed or the changing coastlines of the earth's continents. Nor is the essence of his prophecies a change in the balance of power, a new way of doing medicine, or a new relationship to the Law of Abundance. Instead, *the heart of the Cayce millennium prophecies is a new world about to be born.* It is a world that is so different than what has been experienced for a long time on this planet that some kind of a transitional experience is required. The old patterns of living, the old ways of thinking, are so contrary to what the new must be that a big step for humanity is just ahead. There needs to be some rite of passage.

However, there are various ways to get from where we have

been to where we need to be. All that a psychic or prophet can do is to read the momentum of the present day. In effect, all that Cayce could do was to describe the trends and identify the likeliest among the possible pathways humanity could choose. And in 1932, 1936 and 1941 Cayce kept seeing the same scenario. The momentum of our choices seemed to be taking us on a pathway leading to tremendous earth changes and painful socioeconomic alterations.

Have we stayed on that course since Cayce stopped giving readings? We can only look at our world and guess. The signs do not look very promising. Humanity continues to pollute the earth and to start destructive wars. Surely these are the kinds of activities that alienate us from the earth—from the mother aspect of God. A symbolic way of viewing earth changes, if they literally do happen, is that the earth will shake us to our senses. We will be forced into a new humility and a respect for the forces of nature. We will have to reexamine what we have been doing to the earth and, by consequence, what we have been doing to each other.

However, all of that is only one pathway. Remember the vision. Remember what the prophecy really is: a spiritual rebirth on this planet. A global family. An era of peace and cooperation. And there are many paths to get there. Some of those ways are more catastrophic than earth changes would ever be, such as nuclear war. Others are more "graceful" (that is, full of God's grace). Not that they would be without their pain, because certain things must be surrendered, and there is always discomfort and pain in letting go of old possessions and self-images.

The choice is still with us to select a transitional scenario full of grace. Our primary concern about times of change should be to find such a pathway. We should not be as concerned about whether people believe the Cayce prophecies of earth changes as we are with how people can begin to live with a new millennium consciousness. If sufficient numbers of us will live now the vision of what the world and humanity are to become, then it is quite likely that our collective rite of passage can be survived by most all of humanity. Many of the remaining chapters in this book concern such a hopeful point of view.

There is no better place to start looking for a hopeful view of what's ahead than the category of Cayce's millennium predictions we have not yet considered: prophecies of Christ's return. That is the focus of the next chapter.

Chapter 4

A New Spirituality and the Coming of Christ

The millennium is about many changes, according to the Cayce prophecies—geological, social, political, economic. But in Cayce's vision, no transformation is more central than a spiritual one. The millennium brings a spiritual renewal; and ultimately, according to his predictions, the millennium is about the return of the Christ Spirit directly into human affairs. This is to be widely experienced and recognized sometime around the beginning of the twenty-first century, although there will be signs earlier.

Those signs of the approaching event will increase in frequency as we near 1998. Among the indicators Cayce foresaw would be a new movement for cooperation and respect among the world's religions—something that is in fact happening now. But even greater changes lie just ahead.

The Cayce millennium prophecies unequivocally state that we are on the threshold of a milestone just as spiritually significant as Christ's physical appearance two thousand years ago, an event that is predestined and was known even to the spiritual initiates who constructed the Great Pyramid thousands of years ago. (Later in this chapter we will examine the exact nature of these Cayce interpretations of ancient Egyptian prophecy.)

This Second Coming will not be a physical birth, as it was with Jesus of Nazareth, but instead an event of more global proportions in which people of every faith may find a place. It is the drawing of the universal Christ Spirit in direct relationship with anyone who sincerely seeks it. According to the Cayce millennium prophecies, the early signs of this new beginning shall be experienced by a growing number of people in the last years of the twentieth century.

Prophecies of a Second Coming

Perhaps no vision of a new age is more dramatic than the possibility of a direct, physical interaction of Christ in human affairs—an intervention that would be perceived by all humanity. Nothing better expresses our hope that a new age would include a spiritual renewal for the human family. It is not presented as a certainty in the Cayce readings, nor are there specific details as to timing or appearance. Rather it is a possibility—perhaps even a likelihood.

In the Cayce material on a Second Coming, several principles are especially noteworthy. He clearly thought of Christ as both a universal spirit that could be seen in all world religions *and* as the soul we call Jesus. However, the Christ-like nature of Jesus was attained over many lifetimes of soul development, culminating in Jesus who became one with the Christ Consciousness. In his teachings about the reappearance of Christ, Cayce indicates that any return will involve this same soul that we call Jesus.

When Cayce was asked in 1932 about the Second Coming, he flatly stated that no date could be given. It would not occur until "His enemies and the earth are wholly in subjection to His will, His powers" (#5749–2). That surely sounds like a very high standard for us to meet. Some might even say it's an almost unrealistic expectation for humanity to be anywhere near that state in the foreseeable future. So it's not surprising that the questioner then backed off slightly and asked if this was now a *preparation* period for Christ's return. Cayce responded that it was better understood as a "testing period."

In another instance, Cayce was asked by a small group of seekers in 1933 to interpret the biblical passage that "the day of the Lord is near at hand." Although his answer was filled with biblical images and poetic phrases, he nevertheless seemed to confirm strongly that the return of Christ is quite possible for our own era:

"That as has been promised through the prophets and the sages of old, the time—and half time—has been and is being fulfilled in this day and generation, and that soon there will again appear in the earth that one through whom many will be called to meet those that are preparing the way for His day in the earth. The Lord, then, will come, 'even as ye have seen him go.'" (#262–49)

When the group followed up with a request for a time estimate concerning such an event, they were told that it could happen only when those people who are Christ's devoted followers make the way passable and clear for Him to come. In other words, there is preparatory work to be done from the human side.

The need for efforts to make the way passable is not the result of some inadequacy on the part of Christ. It is not a matter of an inability of Christ to appear in materiality without our help. Instead we might think of it this way: Unless a sufficient portion of humanity lifts itself into a new awareness, then a reappearance of Christ would confuse us or be easily misunderstood by us. Christ will come again only when such an intervention will be truly helpful in the spiritual evolution of which we are a part. It is out of the most profound kind of love that any widescale, directly physical appearance of Christ is delayed.

Perhaps the most remarkable question and answer exchange about Christ's return took place in 1933. A group of people who were seeking to understand more about the Christ Consciousness inquired about the present location of this spiritual being. They even wondered if He might already be on earth in a physical body but unrecognized.

Cayce's answer was that Christ was not currently in a body in the earth dimension. What's more, if a person needed to have a "location" for Him, it was best to understand it to be "in the individual entity," as spirit that can be contacted by anyone who sincerely desires it and who is willing to act in love to make it possible. In other words, if we feel the need to know a "place" where Christ currently resides, it's in a place of spirit that can be contacted as we each go within ourselves.

Finally, Cayce made it clear that he envisioned an actual return. "For, He shall come as ye have seen Him go, in the body He occupied in Galilee. The body that He formed, that was crucified on the cross, that rose from the tomb, that walked by the sea, that appeared to Simon, that appeared to Philip" (#5749–4). This is a very straightforward reference to the resurrected body of Christ reappearing in our own times.

Another group of Cayce prophecies provides a fascinating aspect of his predictions about Christ's return. These predictions are based on Cayce's perception that hidden prophecies are built into the geometric architecture of the Great Pyramid. To decipher them, Cayce stated that the central passageway of the Great Pyramid is like a timeline. This timeline corresponds to the Ascending Passageway and the Grand Gallery passageway, leading up to the King's Chamber. Among the pyramid prophecies is the indication of Christ's return at the turn of the new millennium now upon us. What point in history corresponds precisely to moving into the special room of spiritual initiation, the King's Chamber? According to the Cayce prophecies, it was the period from 1938 to 1958.

What was to be found in the King's Chamber itself? Only an empty sarcophagus. Cayce's interpretation of the empty sarcophagus was that humanity would discover that death is not what we've thought it was. In other words, we would awaken to our connections with the spiritual world, and the continuity of life would become an established fact. "The *interpretation* of death will be made plain" (#5748–6). One can't help but consider how near-death experience research, started in the 1960s, has radically altered our sense of survival.

Interpreting Cayce's Prophecies of a Second Coming

We may well wonder what kind of an expression of Christ we are to expect. What scenario seems most likely? These readings predict that it will not come in the birth of a baby, as Jesus did two thousand years ago. The pattern of incarnation by birth has already been established and doesn't need to be repeated. Instead He will manifest in the very body that He resurrected long ago. Having so purified the flesh body and attuned it to the mind and spirit, Jesus the Christ can manifest that body in any plane or dimension at will.

There are at least three scenarios for His return. One is the spectacular, mass appearance—the Christ seen by millions of people in all His glory. In this scenario the populace of the world is quickly humbled, and the Christ reigns in a spiritual and political sense. Many branches of fundamentalism in Christianity expect some version of this scenario, often coupled with cataclysm and punishments to befall the earth just prior to the reappearance.

A second hypothesis is that Christ will reappear in much the same manner He did just after the first Easter. This scenario involves the direct physical experience of His Presence by individuals and small groups. Recall the way in which Jesus ate fish with the disciples in Galilee just after His resurrection. In this case and in others, He clearly was perceived in a physical way in the outer world.

A third possibility is that a return of Christ will be at nonphysical inner levels of awareness. Already there are individuals who claim to have had such a direct experience, and perhaps the Second

Coming implies a dramatic increase in the number of people who experience this. The inner contact (via meditation, prayer, dreams, etc.) could well be with the resurrected body, mind and spirit of Jesus who became the Christ. Such a personal contact by millions of people would have a dramatic and uplifting effect on the attitudes and life-styles of people worldwide.

Cayce's contemporary, the Austrian philosopher and spiritual scientist Dr. Rudolf Steiner, predicted a return of Christ that is much like the third scenario. Steiner believed that it was Christ manifesting His purified etheric body that we could expect in our own times. To personally meet the etheric Christ, one would have to make sincere efforts to purify and attune his or her conscious-ness—that is, to become more spiritually sensitive. In fact, Steiner even offered a date, predicting that these personal encounters with the etheric Christ would start to happen more and more often, beginning in 1930 (not far from the 1936 date that came up several times in Cayce prophecies).

There is evidence to suggest that such personal encounters with Christ are on the rise. Although they take many forms, some seem to fit the description hinted at by Cayce and explicitly described by Steiner as a kind of extended perception into the spiritual world. For example, in research I conducted with Dr. G. Scott Sparrow for a book he later wrote, *Witness to His Return*, each of us spoke with dozens of individuals for whom the return of Christ was already here—not something still to be awaited.

For example, one man shared with me an extraordinary story of his wife's direct experience with Christ just before her death. It seemed that her consciousness had begun to extend into the spiritual world as her physical body neared death. One day, when a friend came over to visit, she suddenly began to talk to people whom her husband and the friend couldn't see. It was as if she was having a party and greeting her guests, but they were invisible to the others in the room. For some twenty minutes she conversed, speaking and then pausing as if listening to the responses. Finally she began saying good night to her guests, thanking them for having come by to visit.

As his wife's invisible party came to an end, she announced to her husband and to the friend there in the room: "Oh, yes, *He* was here. He told me I was going to die tomorrow. Isn't that wonderful?" The man knew without a doubt that the reference was to Christ, who had come in this vision to tell her of her imminent passing into the spiritual world. In fact, she passed away at 2:00 the next morning.

Edgar Cayce himself from time to time had visionary experiences of Christ which fit the third scenario of how Christ's return might manifest. Here is but one example, recounted by Cayce in a letter to a friend:

"Often I have felt, seen and heard the Master at hand. Just a few days ago I had an experience which I have not even told the folk here. As you say, they are too scary to tell, and we wonder at ourselves when we attempt to put them into words, whether we are to believe our own ears, or if others feel we are exaggerating or drawing on our imagination; but to us indeed they are often that which we feel if we hadn't experienced we could not have gone on.

"The past week I have been quite 'out of the running,' but Wednesday afternoon when going into my little office or den for the 4:45 meditation, as I knelt by my couch I had the following experience: First a light gradually filled the room with a golden glow, that seemed to be very exhilarating, putting me in a buoyant state. I felt as if I were being given a healing. Then, as I was about to give the credit to members of our own [prayer] group who meet at this hour for meditation (as I felt each and every one of them were praying for and with me), HE came. He stood before me for a few minutes in all the glory that He must have appeared in to the three on the Mount. Like yourself I heard the voice of my Jesus say, 'Come unto me and rest.'" (supplement to #281-13)

Whichever scenario or interpretation of the Second Coming seems most likely to you, an important factor to keep in mind is the necessity for being open to the new. We must avoid repeating what happened in Jesus' time. Christ will come again only in the spirit of that which is propelling humanity's evolution forward, and hence will appear as something unexpected and new. In *Revelation: The Birth of a New Age*, philosopher David Spangler states this beautifully. It is a principle worth keeping in mind as we work to make the way passable for the coming again of the Christ into the physical plane. Spangler asks us to remember that Jesus faced rejection from many of his contemporaries, largely because he didn't fit their expectations of what a messiah ought to be. Those who spurned him couldn't see the depth and enormity of what he brought to humanity. With this in mind, Spangler warns that "the Christ manifestation for this new age could go unrecognized and rejected by many who are thinking of a Second Coming as a repetition and reinforcement of the past. We are in a new age."

The Christ Spirit in These Times of Change

Our ideas of a Second Coming usually focus on dramatic scenarios in which this high spiritual being Cayce called "Jesus who became the Christ" returns in such a way that believers and nonbelievers alike can directly encounter Him. But perhaps there are other manifestations of a Second Coming—not necessarily ones that replace this kind of direct contact but still broaden the possibilities for how these prophecies will be fulfilled.

In fact, we can look at the trends and events around us right now and find among them many hopeful signs. Although it's certainly more fashionable to focus on the negative and disturbing side of current events, we can just as readily find indicators that something very good is afoot.

Let's consider just a few such movements on the modern scene. In each one we can find key elements of the universal Christ Consciousness—as Cayce's spiritual philosophy defines it—coming to life in extraordinary new ways. Could these be the first signs of the worldwide spiritual revitalization that Cayce's millennium prophecies suggest? Like the first crocuses of March, might these trends be the harbingers of a new sort of planetary culture? If so, then they are every bit as much a part of the Second Coming as any rematerialization of Jesus. Why? Simply because a return of Christ must this time be to stimulate a fuller expression of the Christ-like ways in human affairs. In Cayce's estimation, there's no need for a so-called Second Coming just to bring mankind additional information or teachings. We already received the Gospel—the good news about a whole new way of understanding spiritual growth and the redemption of the soul—two thousand years ago. Now the cutting edge of any fresh involvement of Christ with humanity must be in the arena of *application*.

The movements described below are simply two examples. Each of us can probably think of other modern events and initiatives that are equally illustrative of the Christ Spirit coming into bold new ways of expression.

Christ as Mediator. One great image of Christ is as the force or impulse that "stands between." Cayce put it this way, referring to the role of Christ: ". . . He who stands between those influences of good and evil, the crossroads of choice, that every one and every soul each day must cross . . ." (#683–2). Theology has for centuries seen Christ as the redemptive middle ground between the spiritual and the physical, between God and humankind. Cayce echoes that principle with his assertion that "Only in Christ do the extremes meet."

But all that seems rather far off and abstract when we're confronted by a chaotic and contentious world. Perhaps we sense the need for spiritual redemption, but too many other problems get in the way, particularly struggles with other people. What does "Christ as Mediator" have to do with a landlord-tenant dispute, two state governments bickering over water rights, or a messy child custody battle between divorcing parents? That's the stuff of which daily life is made.

Remarkably there is, indeed, a social movement growing very rapidly to bring this consciousness of "mediator" into human affairs, especially problem solving. It rarely carries with it any kind of religious language and few (if any) of its practitioners probably think directly of the Christ Consciousness as they carry out their challenging work. But if we look carefully at the spirit and the purposes of this movement, we can immediately recognize a new model for human relations—one in which problems are resolved not by force, but instead with mutual respect and the search for common ground. And if we broaden our vision of what a Second Coming might really mean—if we look at our times with the eyes that the Cayce millennium prophecies encourage us to use—then we're likely to see this mediation movement as a direct expression of the Christ Spirit, especially in the sense of Christ as a middle way between extreme positions.

In this process, parties meet with a trained mediator who assists them in reaching fair, informed decisions to resolve the issues before them. The mediator is not the judge of the conflict. He or she has received extensive training in ways to be an effective bridge and clarifier. The consciousness of the mediator serves as a point where the divergent attitudes and needs can meet and where the parties can explore options in a nonthreatening way. Truly such a person is playing a redemptive role—not as cosmic as the theological one of Christ as redeemer and middle ground between God and humanity, but nevertheless a powerful expression of how the Christ Spirit comes to life in everyday human events.

What does this modern mediation movement have to offer our society? Besides being less costly than litigation or warfare, mediation offers participants a great deal of flexibility in reaching agreements that are tailored to their special circumstances. In addition, mediation can be concluded much more quickly than litigation or armed confrontation, and the parties can avoid the usual hostilities that accompany adversarial court proceedings or international brinkmanship.

For family or community relations problems, mediation sessions are usually designed to be informal, private and voluntary. Unlike litigation in which the sole objective is to "win," mediation emphasizes different goals: communication, understanding and problem solving. The participants meet with this neutral third party to explore the issues and problems that are important to them. The participants, not the mediator, make the ultimate decisions that will affect their lives. The mediator's role is to skillfully assist the parties in identifying significant issues and needs. Then the mediator leads the parties to a resolution of the conflict by brainstorming options, assessing the implications of each option and finalizing an agreement.

Through the mediation process, participants have the opportunity to create custom-made agreements with provisions that are tailored to meet each individual's needs. It is no surprise that mediated agreements are statistically much more likely to be observed and followed than are court-imposed orders. Moreover, through the mediation process, parties have the added benefit of learning how to communicate constructively with one another, so that their future and ongoing relationship may be less stressful and more productive.

Almost any conflict can be mediated, and it's reasonable to hope that in a twenty-first century culture guided by the Christ Spirit, mediation will become the norm for problem solving in human relations—at personal, community, and international levels.

Christ in Interfaith Dialogue. Cayce's millennium prophecies have a deeply ecumenical spirit. Although many of his predictions seem to carry a certain theological slant—after all, he speaks of a return of Christ, not Buddha, Krishna, or Mohammed—the deeper import of his millennium prophecies is fundamentally bigger than any single religion. We must recall that he was making these prophetic statements to people who were themselves rooted in a single religious tradition. For the most part that was a rather conservative, Protestant Christianity of the early twentieth century in the South. Cayce started from that point, then challenged his listeners (and us, today) to a broader vision of what's just ahead.

The return of the Christ Consciousness directly into human affairs will require a pluralistic vision of faith and spirituality. Here are but two examples of Cayce's vision of a planetary spirituality that is not limited by the terminology or doctrines of one religion.

First, we can look back at an incident in Edgar Cayce's own life. His work as a professional clairvoyant was not always very successful, at least from a financial standpoint. He depended upon membership dues from individuals who joined his organization in order to get a reading, but there were periods in which requests for readings were meager. At one point in the spring of 1935 Cayce's supporters asked for a special reading specifically on the question of fund-raising.

A key concern was how to reach their potential audience. How should Cayce's work be described? In the very first question they posed for this special reading, they asked if Cayce's work should be portrayed as direct pronouncements from Christ. Admittedly, for many of us who now look back at that question sixty years later, it seems bold—even a bit presumptuous. However, it was a sincere inquiry on the part of some of Cayce's most ardent followers. They not only felt that Christ was the source of his inspiration, but that it was crucial to label the readings exactly that way.

The answer given that day was a reflection of a more universal and ecumenical spirit: Don't set up limitations. Try to be all things to all people; meet seekers where they are. To get focused exclusively on a name behind these teachings means to limit interested people who might have personal difficulties with certain terminology. Focus instead on the universality of the Creator. "Be ye all things to all men; thereby ye may save the more. For he that declares as a name, in a name, save in the universality of the Father, limits the ability of the seeker . . ." (#254–85). In other words, Cayce encouraged finding a common ground from which seekers of all persuasions could meet.

A second illustration of Cayce's interfaith ideal is found in the sort of advice he often gave individuals who had adopted too narrow a picture of spirituality. To emphasize the fundamental oneness of humanity's spiritual quest, Cayce tried to bring his hearers back to basics. There is only one God, no matter what name or label is used. For example, one young woman, a student from Sarah Lawrence College, was reminded, "For whether they be Greek, Parthenian [Parthian], Jew or Gentile—whether they be of Mohammed, Confucius, or even Shinto or On or Mu—the Lord, the God, is ONE!" (#1494–1).

Of course, Cayce is only one of many twentieth century philosophers, theologians, and creative thinkers who have seen the importance of the ecumenical spirit. Surely, the interfaith dialogue that we see in our midst as the millennium approaches is a sign of something extraordinary in human history—perhaps even part of the blossoming of the universal Christ Consciousness.

No less a figure than the renowned British historian Arnold Toynbee observed the significance of pluralistic vision. Speculating about what might be seen five hundred years from now as *the* most important event of the twentieth century, he didn't select the splitting of the atom or the human gene, or any war or technological achievement. Rather, he predicted historians of the distant future would recognize as the most significant development of the century a spiritual movement: the meeting of the wisdom traditions of Buddhism and the East with Western Judeo-Christian faith.

The Parliament of World Religions, held in Chicago in 1993, is surely a sign of this movement. At that meeting, more than sixty-five hundred participants from virtually every religious tradition on the planet gathered to look for common bonds. It was a coming together of East and West; of North and South.

One of their central tasks was the shaping of a set of ethical standards that could unite humanity. Not looking for a common set of religious beliefs or devotional practices, they instead focused on the possibility for a mutually acceptable set of behavioral standards in which all men and women could participate for the good of humanity and the earth itself. The declaration of this parliament has been published as *A Global Ethic*. In its preamble, this description of the process was offered: "As was only to be expected, this declaration provoked vigorous discussion during the parliament. However, the welcome thing is that at a time when so many religions are entangled in political conflicts, indeed bloody wars, representatives of very different religions, great and small, endorsed this declaration with their signatures on behalf of countless believers on this earth."

A Personal Reflection on Christ's Return

To come back to a point made earlier in this chapter: There's no need for Christ to return merely to bring additional teachings. We already have the information we need. Our big requirement is to find a way to live in keeping with the spirit of those teachings. The focus of any fresh involvement of Christ with humanity must be in the arena of *application.*

This point was made vivid to me in a profound personal experience many years ago. It came just as I had finished my college education and was contemplating making a commitment to spend my professional career working directly with the Cayce material. It had already touched me deeply with its vision of these special times in which we live, especially in regard to the return of Christ in my own lifetime.

I joined forty-nine other members of the organization that Edgar Cayce had founded many years before his death—the Association for Research and Enlightenment—for a month-long tour of places of spiritual significance throughout Europe and the Middle East.

One place that I especially looked forward to visiting was the Great Pyramid. I had carefully read the Cayce material about Jesus and pondered the idea that He had traveled to Egypt for schooling in the esoteric traditions before He began His three-year ministry. Cayce describes it as a process of spiritual initiation and indicates that Jesus experienced a kind of final initiation in the King's Chamber of the Great Pyramid. And so, in my twenty-two-year-old youthful enthusiasm, I was ready to be an initiate, too. I was prepared to go to this same spot and hopefully have some sort of transformative experience.

Egypt was not the first stop on our tour, so I had plenty of time for the anticipation to build as we traveled. Finally we arrived in Cairo, and on our second day there, we took the bus out to the Giza Plateau just beyond the city.

After that forty-five minute ride, we arrived at the Great Pyramid. To stand beside it for the first time is an awe-inspiring experience. Although it is not as tall as other familiar landmarks, such as the Washington Monument, its sheer size and volume is staggering. And the thought that it was built with human labor and archaic tools thousands of years ago defies imagination.

The leader of our group gave the official at the entrance a little extra money, which would provide our group with some private time in the King's Chamber. The fifty of us went in single file. As mentioned earlier, much of the climb inside is along an Ascending Passageway, which slants upward and is so low that you can move through it only in a crouched position. Finally, the structure opens up into the Grand Gallery, still relatively narrow but with a very high ceiling. The ascent through the Grand Gallery leads into the King's Chamber, a room just the right size for the fifty of us to line the perimeter of the stone room. We all sat down and leaned back against the cool, hard surface.

After a short period of discussion from our leader to remind us of the significance of this spot, we had a lengthy group meditation. This was what I had come for. I was hoping for a powerful experience—something mystical perhaps. I knew I wasn't alone in my desires. Most of the group shared my feelings.

Unfortunately, I was so excited that I couldn't get still and quiet, and so my meditation time didn't seem very successful. My enthusiasm ironically had become an obstacle. When the twenty minutes of silence ended, I was disappointed but nevertheless profoundly impressed by this extraordinary place.

We retraced our steps in departing. Finally, back out in the bright Egyptian sunlight, our guide announced that we had about two hours of free time. Among our options were a short walk to the nearby Sphinx or an equally short walk over to one of the two other pyramids nearby. Although I was certainly eager to see the Sphinx, I decided to wait and finish some other business first. I had the sense that I had not yet received what I had come to Giza to experience at the Great Pyramid. So while my companions scattered, I walked around to the back side of the Great Pyramid and began to climb its exterior. When it was originally constructed, a smooth, limestone sheathing covered the huge stones which layer-upon-layer create its immense size. But long ago those finishing stones were stripped away, and all that remains are large construction stones that create a steplike appearance when seen up close. It was easy to climb, and within a couple of minutes I was seventy-five feet up the side. I found a nice shelf about two feet by three feet and sat down cross-legged to meditate some more.

Rarely in my meditation times had I ever experienced something remarkable. In fact, my special inner experiences had usually been—and continue to be—in my dreams, especially dreams that came immediately upon falling back asleep after a meditation at three or four o'clock in the morning. However, this day, sitting in meditation on the side of the Great Pyramid, "something happened."

Suddenly, as I sat in silence with my eyes closed, trying to keep my attention one-pointed, I saw a scene. It was as if I were looking at something that opened up in my forehead. However, it wasn't mystical or transcendent. I saw myself sitting in a business meeting! At the time of this experience I was only twenty-two and didn't have a job with any organization—but I did have hopes of someday working for the Cayce organization in Virginia Beach. In this meditation experience I saw myself in a roundtable business discussion at that very headquarters center, and I "knew" my identity was a staff member.

I listened intently as I watched this meeting unfold. I had a strong sense that everyone in the room had the same *ideal,* but I quickly heard that each person had a different *idea* about how to get some particular task accomplished. There was argument and some spirited tension. I felt myself being drawn in, and I was about to speak up and lobby for my own point of view.

Then, unexpectedly, I heard a voice in my mind that made me stop and surrender all intentions to get caught up in the argument. The voice began, "Be still." I felt my emotions become free from the entanglements of the business meeting. Then this voice of wisdom went on. "The real work of this organization—as it plays its part in this new millennium and the coming again of Christ— is not so much that conferences would be held, books written or lectures given, as important as those things may be. The real work and purpose is simply this: *That a new way of being, with each other, would be born into the earth."* And with those words I suddenly came back to normal consciousness sitting on the side of the Great Pyramid.

Undoubtedly those images and the accompanying words were especially for me, and they've stayed vividly etched in my mind and ideals. Each of us has his or her own way of understanding what the Christ Spirit is all about in these times, and this was my way of catching the vision for myself. But maybe it speaks to others as well.

Since that day in 1972, my own career has unfolded in such a way that public speaking and book writing have been central ingredients of my work. Perhaps this inner wisdom—this meditative voice—recognized well in advance that I would have tendencies to overemphasize them from time to time. The *form* of Christ's work today (be it lectures, books, or anything else) should never blind us from the authentic *spirit*. And in today's changing world, that spirit is perhaps best described as a new social art, a new way of being present and involved with each other. That, more than any other characteristic, may be the way we recognize the return of Christ.

Chapter 5

~

MODERN GEOLOGY
EVALUATES CAYCE'S
MILLENNIUM PROPHECIES

Some of Cayce's millennium prophecies for earth changes seem fantastic—almost unbelievable. Others don't sound too different from the warnings of mainstream geology. And if we look carefully at the modern scientific understanding of the origins of the physical world, we discover the central role of cataclysmic changes—just the sort of changes Cayce indicated to be not only part of our distant past but also our near future.

Even though mainstream scientists don't generally agree with Cayce's timetable for the future, they know that *we ourselves* are the result of tremendous catastrophic processes in the past. Simply put, we wouldn't be here today if there hadn't once been extraordinary cataclysms. Of course, that in no way provides evidence that immense changes are coming in the next few years. But it does call upon us to recognize just how necessary catastrophic change is to growth and evolution as we know it.

For example, according to scientific wisdom, the granddaddy of all such events was the Big Bang, some ten to twenty *billion* years ago. It set in motion the creation of the entire universe. Since the Big Bang, creation has continued on a grand scale with the formation and death of entire solar systems. And moving from the cosmic to the personal scale, the atoms of calcium within our bones and the iron in our blood were created within crucibles of stellar catastrophes. These elements were created long ago during the energy release of a dying star—a supernova, in which the star collapses suddenly into a dense neutron star. These supernova events each release the equivalent energy of the entire output of our own sun over its projected ten-billion-year life span, all released in an event that lasts just seconds. Science tells us that all heavy atoms in the universe are created in such a way, then dispersed and made available for further creation. Our own physical bodies are, in fact, made from old star material, sent drifting through space billions of years ago. Without such cataclysms, we couldn't be here today as physical beings.

With that humbling view of history in mind, we can look at the Cayce millennium prophecies in a bigger framework. As human beings living on this planet at the end of the twentieth century, we are the end-product of many, many cataclysmic changes. It seems reasonable to expect that more will be part of our future.

Consulting an Expert

It's a challenging task to correlate the predictions of Cayce about potential cataclysms to what mainstream science considers possible. I knew I needed an expert to help me sort out and interpret these geological predictions. My search landed me on the doorstep of John Peterson. And the more I got to know of his background, it became obvious to me that he was the most qualified person to help me sort out a scientifically responsible interpretation of Cayce's earth change material.

Peterson's experience includes bachelors' and master's degrees in geology, more than twenty years of professional scientific work, and his current position as a geologist for the County of San Diego, right in the heart of earthquake-vulnerable portions of California. Very little garnered from his graduate school training resembled

Cayce's extraordinary ideas about the earth's immediate future. But I found him to be totally informed about Cayce's predictions, having thirty years of personal involvement with the Cayce material:

"I've watched and waited for catastrophic earth changes ever since I first read the Cayce millennium prophecies when I was seventeen. I remember thinking in high school that I wouldn't have to study for an upcoming math test because the 'big one' would come and change the world."

Peterson was easy to learn from. He wasn't defensive about the biases of scientific geology. Nor was he gullible about the possible fallibility of Cayce, whom he clearly admires. We spent many hours discussing the pros and cons of taking the Cayce millennium prophecies at face value. And he shared with me a lengthy article he wrote to analyze the similarities and differences between Cayce and traditional geologic theory.

First he reminded me that historically there is ample record of disastrous natural changes. Sometimes human beings have luckily been out of harm's way; other times, huge losses of life have resulted. Human history would not have proceeded as it has without many natural calamities. Some amazing statistics can be found in *Catastrophic Episodes in Earth History* by Claude C. Albritton, Jr. For example, floods have killed approximately 4.9 million people in the years 1642 to 1973. In one extraordinarily devastating month, August 1931, floods along the Yellow River in China killed an estimated 3.5 million individuals! And in the thirty-five years immediately after World War II, an estimated 1.2 million people died in natural disasters. Within the United States the economic toll from natural disasters averages $52 billion per year.

The power of the earth is especially evident when its surface changes dramatically and rapidly. When Mount St. Helens erupted, it destroyed a two-hundred-square-mile area and blasted thirteen hundred feet off the top of the mountain. The event affected the entire northwestern portion of the United States with volcanic ash fallout. However, this effect was small compared to some previous volcanic eruptions which have left a geological record.

In addition to volcanic eruptions, earthquakes have destroyed large regions and have killed many millions of people. Some examples from recent years:

Date	Location	Magnitude	Deaths	Damage (in millions $)
1995	Kobe, Japan	7.2	4,800	30,000
1994	Northridge, CA	6.8	61	20,000
1993	Marharashtra, India	6.4	30,000	280
1990	Luzon, Philippines	7.7	1,621	2,000
1990	Northwestern Iran	7.7	40,000	7,000
1989	San Francisco	6.9	62	6,000
1988	Northwest Armenia	6.8	55,000	14,000
1985	Mexico City	8.1	4,200	4,000
1976	Tangshan, China	8.2	242,000	5,600
1970	Northern Peru	7.7	66,794	500

As frightening as those kinds of figures may be, earthquakes aren't the only killers. Seismic sea waves, commonly referred to as tidal waves, also have changed many lives and nations and destroyed many cities and regions. The 1896 seismic sea wave that hit Sanrika, Japan, killed an estimated 26,000 people. When the volcano Krakatau exploded in 1883 in the East Indies, it produced a sea wave 115 feet high, which washed away 165 villages and killed more than 36,000 people. That wave was recorded around the world and was even detected in the English Channel. Although the Cayce prophecies don't specifically refer to seismic sea waves, they would undoubtedly play a big role if earthquakes occurred on the scale that he predicted.

Plate Tectonics

As we got into an analysis of the intricacies of how the earth goes through major alterations, I realized that I had to learn the basics (or "relearn" them, since I vaguely remembered having to memorize these details for high school earth science tests). I had only an obscure notion of the mechanism behind tidal waves, volcanos, and earthquakes, so I asked for more information.

First, Peterson gave me a brief review of plate tectonics—or, as *Webster's New World Dictionary* puts it, "the study of the earth's crustal structure and the forces that produce changes in it." Peterson explained that the surface of the earth consists of ten major segments or "plates" and many smaller ones. Plates are approximately fifty miles thick and span many thousands of square miles. In fact, the entire United States is but a portion of the North American Plate, which extends from the middle of the Atlantic Ocean to the San Andreas Fault in California.

These plates move about independently. And as they move, energy is stored and released, causing the earth changes that affect us. Three basic types of interface occur between earth plates: (1) collision as two plates strike each other; (2) separation between two plates as they move away from each other; and (3) horizontal movement between two plates as they slip past each other. He went on to describe how plate movement can generate many types of earth changes; some of the changes we might expect in the future include (1) volcanic eruptions, (2) earthquakes, and (3) seismic sea waves (tidal waves).

Volcanos

Volcanos can result when one plate is being pushed down under another plate. The energy produced when the plates slip past each other melts the surrounding rock, which then rises to the surface as molten lava flowing from the volcano. In Washington and Oregon, the Cascade volcanos (and notably Mount St. Helens) are familiar examples. These volcanos were created by the downward movement of a small plate under the North American Plate, and their periodic eruptions are evidence of continuing plate movement.

Volcanic activity may also be caused by two plates moving apart. Hot melted rock (magma) flows up into the resulting gap between plates and rises to the surface. Volcanos generated by this type of plate movement are restricted to certain zones on the earth—for example, along the Mid-Atlantic Ridge which divides the American Plates from the African and Eurasian Plates. This zone has a high number of active volcanos. Those in Iceland are good examples. Here the island is actually being split in two, and new crust is continually being generated.

One other cause of volcanos can be observed in the Hawaiian Islands and Yellowstone National Park. These areas seem to be created by "hot spots" in the mantle of the earth—that is, areas of intense heat within the earth's mantle which are located under a moving plate. A hot spot gives rise to volcanic activity directly above it and builds a row of volcanos as the plate moves across the relatively stable hot spot. The Hawaiian Island chain is an example of this with its distinct line of submerged and exposed volcanos extending past Midway Island. This chain was created as the Pacific Plate moved toward the northwest over the hot spot.

Each type of volcanic eruption has its own particular characteristics. Variations in the rock in different areas contribute to two primary kinds of eruptions: the explosive eruptions, such as those in the Northwest, and the relatively quiet ones, such as those in the Hawaiian chain. In the Hawaiian Islands, the melted rock that is extruded is more fluid and contains less vaporized water than the magma in the Pacific Northwest. The volcanos in the Pacific Northwest are more dangerous for the surrounding population because of the explosive type of volcanic eruption. Mount St. Helens was an excellent example from recent history of what that explosive power can do.

Earthquakes

One of the most violent earthquakes ever recorded in North America occurred 5:36 P.M. on Good Friday, March 27, 1964. By the time the earth had stopped shaking, an estimated 77,000 square miles of Alaska had been deformed. The earthquake had caused $300,000,000 in property damage and killed 130 people *in a land that was almost deserted!* For over thousands of square miles, the shaking was so severe that people were thrown from their feet and some became ill from motion sickness. It's not just Edgar Cayce who is predicting that something like this may soon occur to *highly populated* California and Japan. It's also those geologists who specialize in movements of the earth's crust—the seismologists.

Earthquakes are geophysical events caused by a release of energy as one land mass moves against or past another. Plate movement is slow, normally not exceeding several inches per year. But as the years go by, the potential energy accumulates until it exceeds the amount of friction holding the rocks together. At this point an earthquake occurs along a fault or fracture in the rocks. The quake releases the stored energy in the form of the earth being shaken. Following an earthquake, the energy is again slowly stored up, and a new cycle begins.

Along the San Andreas Fault zone, hundreds of earthquakes happen every day. Most are very small and cannot be felt by the people living in the area. In such areas, the amount of friction that is holding the fault from slipping is small, and because of this the amount of energy that stores up is also small. Hollister, California, located on the San Andreas Fault, is known for frequent small daily tremors. In such an area, a large, destructive event is unlikely, whereas in an area like San Francisco a great amount of friction appears to be holding the fault together, blocking movement. In spite of the 1989 earthquake, there is still considerable destructive potential stored up. Now, when a major earthquake does happen, it is likely to be similar in magnitude to the devastating 1906 quake.

The San Andreas Fault area is a major system because it separates the North American Plate from the Pacific Plate. The Pacific Plate is moving toward the Northwest relative to the North American Plate at an average rate of four to five inches per year. It was here that Peterson dispelled for me the popular notion of California "disappearing into the sea." The history of this type of plate movement, he said, shows that California and the West Coast are not likely to "fall off" into the Pacific; it might move northward, but large-scale *vertical* movements are extremely *unlikely*.

This type of earthquake zone (horizontal slippage of one plate past another) normally produces shallow-focused earthquakes, that is, of a depth of less than one mile. These shallow-focused quakes are responsible for about three-quarters of the total energy released from earthquakes throughout the earth. In other areas, earthquakes occur at depths of up to 350 miles. Deep-focused quakes are prevalent along plate boundaries wherein one plate is being pushed *under* another. In such areas, earthquakes are occurring along the margin of the two plates as they collide. For example, along the western edge of the South American continent, the continental plate is moving toward the west, colliding with a large oceanic plate in the Southern Pacific. As this occurs, the heavy, dense rocks of oceanic plate are forced down under the lighter rocks of the South American Plate, triggering a high number of earthquakes. The 1964 Alaskan earthquake was a result of this type of activity as the Pacific Plate was pushed under a portion of the North American Plate.

In addition to earthquakes along plate margins, quakes can also occur *within* plates, far from the margins. These types of earthquakes are normally small and infrequent, although they have occurred in several locations within the United States. One of the largest was the great 1811 New Madrid, Missouri, earthquake, which caused considerable damage in the area and was felt as far away as Washington, D.C. This type of quake is thought to be caused by localized forces related to readjustments within the rocks. This made me think of some of the Cayce prophecies for earth changes in the southeastern part of the United States, for a redirecting of the Mississippi River, and for sudden changes in Europe.

The magnitude of a quake is measured in one of two ways: (1) a direct measurement of the energy released or (2) the relative degree of movement felt by people in the area and the amount of damage produced. The Richter scale is the most commonly used method of measuring and comparing earthquakes and was developed by Charles Richter in 1935. It is a direct measure of the energy released and an indirect measure of the amount of damage produced by a quake. As the rocks are shaken and deformed during an earthquake, they transmit vibratory waves that can be monitored as they reach the surface of the earth. The Richter scale method measures these wave heights as recorded by a seismograph (a machine developed in Germany at the turn of the twentieth century and designed to monitor earth movement). Because the size of earthquakes varies enormously, the scale is based on the logarithm of the height of recorded earthquake waves on the seismograph. An increase of one unit on the scale indicates a *ten times* increase in the earthquake waves; the amount of *released energy* is increased *thirty-three times*. The Richter scale is open-ended, with no upper or lower limit. However, practically speaking, the upper limit to the magnitude of earthquakes is determined by the strength of the rocks, and it is presently believed that 9.5 is about the largest magnitude possible, because most rocks are not capable of storing greater amounts of energy. The largest quakes measured in modern times were of this magnitude, in Chile in 1960.

The magnitude of an earthquake is measured at its focal point, or epicenter, defined as the point on the earth's surface directly above the initial point of movement. Normally most damage is done at or around the epicenter because this is the point closest to the energy release. Less and less damage occurs as you move farther from this point.

Seismic Sea Waves

Seismic sea waves (or tidal waves) are an aspect of earth changes that many students of the Cayce prophecies have overlooked. The term "tidal wave" (sometimes referred to by the Japanese word, "tsunami") is misleading, because tides have nothing to do with this type of wave.

Seismic sea waves are generated by a large pulse of energy either from an earthquake, a large landslide or a volcanic eruption. In everyday ocean movements, a typical wave's impact extends downward no more than one hundred feet. But with a seismic sea wave, the influence extends many thousands of feet below the surface. Because of this, the wave in the open ocean is normally only several feet high, but as it reaches shallow water, the energy becomes focused upward, causing the wave to grow higher. The largest seismic sea waves have been recorded at heights exceeding one hundred fifty feet! Just imagine standing on a beach and seeing an approaching wave as high as a fifteen-story office building.

In the open ocean, seismic sea waves travel between four hundred to four hundred fifty miles per hour and can cross an ocean basin within half a day! While traveling on the open sea, the wave loses little energy; however, when it hits land, the energy is then quickly released, creating the coastal devastation commonly associated with this type of earth change.

Even though a seismic sea wave might reach a peak of one hundred feet or more, it usually doesn't travel very far inland. Damage is restricted to the extreme lowlands and river mouths. But think about all the dense population centers along coasts. A large seismic sea wave could have a tremendous impact on an entire country.

Scientific Probabilities of Cataclysms

Modern geology and seismology know all about these destructive events. It's much harder to know the likelihoods and probabilities of their occurrence.

I asked Peterson if mainstream science has any scenarios as catastrophic as many of the Cayce millennium prophecies sound. He could think of only two situations that might cause worldwide havoc: a meteor impact and a special type of volcanic eruption called a "collapse caldera."

Consider, for example, the scientific speculation concerning the destruction of the dinosaurs from the impact of a meteor. Computer simulations of the impact of a ten kilometer object indicate that the lofted dust would circle the earth. The planet would become so dark that for a period of months, you literally could not see your hand in front of your face. The lack of sunlight would halt photosynthesis, causing a catastrophic collapse of the food chain worldwide.

This event would also produce extremely low global temperatures and would lead to the extinction of many species. It is probable that such events have occurred in the past and produced many extinctions which have been left in the geological record. What's more, one has only to look at the surface of the Moon to see such impact craters.

The second potential cause, a so-called "collapse caldera," refers to a volcanic eruption so strong that a majority of the mountain is thrown up into the atmosphere. Following such an event, the mountain collapses in on itself, leaving a large hole. Crater Lake in Oregon is an example. The most impressive such eruption was in 1815 on Tambora, an island south of Borneo. It ejected twenty cubic miles of material into the atmosphere, eighty times the amount from Mount St. Helens. The resultant "year without a summer" included worldwide crop failures, a typhus epidemic throughout Europe, food riots in France, and thousands of starvation deaths. But even Tambora is small compared to what geologists know is possible. Approximately seventy-five thousand years ago the Toba caldera in Sumatra erupted with ten times the power of the 1815 event.

Seismologists, of course, know that earth changes aren't merely a matter of waiting for one of these extraordinary events. There will be earthquakes *every* year, an estimated twelve million of them, about one hundred of which are dangerous and disruptive to society. The vast majority of these earthquakes will occur in narrowly defined zones, concentrated along the plate boundaries. As seismologists carefully study these boundaries, they formulate probability figures, especially for many of the most vulnerable spots. For example, there is a 50–50 chance of the Hayward Fault near San Francisco producing a 7.5 quake in the next fifty years. Such estimations are only a best guess, and they're complex because they consider location, timing, and intensity.

Here are some examples of the probability figures prepared by the scientists with the U.S. Geological Survey for earthquake-vulnerable California.

Area	Magnitude Quake	Probability in 30 years
North CA coast	8.0	less than 10%
San Francisco	7.0	25%
Just south of S.F.	7.0	less than 5%
Parkfield, CA	6.0	greater than 90%
Coachella Valley	7.5	40%
Northern L.A.	7.0	greater than 60%
San Diego	6.0	less than 20%

The small probability listed for the area directly south of San Francisco is due to the energy release from recent quakes in that area. Many other vulnerable areas can be added to the list. For example, the western portions of Oregon and Washington state are the sites of converging plates and are susceptible to an earthquake as strong as the low to mid-9s, although it is very difficult to calculate odds on that event. However, geologic evidence suggests major earthquake activity about every four hundred years, and there has been none in the past two hundred fifty years.

New Madrid, Missouri, (near the convergence of Missouri, Arkansas, Kentucky, and Tennessee) experienced three extremely powerful earthquakes early in the 19th century—probably reaching at least 8.0 in magnitude. The probability of a 7.0 or greater quake in the next fifty years is put at more than twenty percent.

Local geological officials in Utah estimate that a 6.5 quake has a twenty percent chance of striking along the Wasatch Fault near Salt Lake City in the next fifty years. And there is a fifty percent chance of a 6.3 quake in eastern Massachusetts in the next two hundred years.

The odds for Japan are considerably more ominous. In the last one hundred years, sixteen earthquakes of magnitude 6.5 or greater have hit this nation. The islands of Honshu and Shikoku are especially vulnerable. In the next twenty years, the most vulnerable twenty percent of the land mass of Japan has a nearly one hundred percent probability of another 6.5 or greater quake. The remaining eighty percent of the land areas range from ten to fifty percent probability of such a quake in those same years.

Assessing the Cayce Prophecies

With all this background information clearer in my mind, John Peterson and I turned our attention to the Cayce earth change predictions. How likely were these events, I wanted to know. If viewed by mainstream geology, are they within the realm of possibility?

Peterson first tried to emphasize a basic principle: the dynamic quality of the earth. "Our planet is thought to be 4.4 to 5 billion years old. However, the oldest known rocks are at most 3.7 billion years old. This means that all the earth materials have been recycled, as Mother Earth continues to move and live," he said. "This will continue into the future. In spite of what some people believe,

I'm of the opinion that the earth's movements *aren't* to punish humanity for being bad. Mother Earth has to move to cleanse herself, as she recycles all her materials."

So, are we now at a time of such a major "cleansing"? I wondered. This question took us back to some of Peterson's own personal history as a student of the Cayce millennium prophecies. "In my late teenage years, having just discovered Cayce, I was sure that the earth changes were imminent. And even years later, after finishing my graduate education in geology, I was still rather expectant that these catastrophes were coming. But as time passed, and I became more and more familiar with seismology, I began to have some questions and doubts about what Cayce had said. My inner feelings indicated that there was an even bigger story than the interpretations of Cayce I had read. I had to go back and reread very carefully the seventeen detailed readings that Cayce gave on the subject."

First Peterson found evidence that Cayce had some skill at clairvoyantly picking up geological trends and future events. He cited two examples: First was Cayce's prediction from April 1932 that Mount Etna would become active and serve as a kind of warning sign that world changes might be imminent.

"Mount Etna, located on the eastern flank of Sicily, is one of a number of large active volcanos which exist in the Mediterranean Sea region," Peterson told me. "The plate tectonics in this region are very complex with a number of small tectonic plates which are aggressively interacting, caught between the Eurasian and African Plates.

"Documented historic activity in Mount Etna goes all the way back to 1500 B.C. when eruptions from the mountain drove the Sican tribe from eastern Sicily. During those years after Cayce's prediction was made, right up to 1942, the mountain was noted for persistent summit activity. A definitive book on the mountain's history, entitled *Mount Etna* by Chester, Duncan, Guest, and Kilburn, notes that right up to September 1933 explosive activity in the central crater of the volcano had built up a small cone. Another part of the volcano was especially active in September and October 1935, and then again intermittently between March 1936 and September 1938. The central crater area then became active again between June 1939 and mid-1942."

All this seemed to suggest that Cayce was on to something, at least in terms of this ancient volcano stirring back to life. Of course, whether or not it was truly an indicator of worldwide changes about to happen was still an open question.

The second example Peterson found of Cayce's clairvoyant skill concerned something closer to home: New York. His in-depth study of Cayce's predictions uncovered some interesting evidence to support the prophecies that New York might be vulnerable to earth changes. When asked in 1932 about the prospects of major earth changes for North America, Cayce sounded an ominous warning for highly populated east coast areas. Although stating that they would eventually be felt throughout the country in a minor or major way, the "greater change" would be along the North Atlantic seaboard. "Watch New York! And Connecticut, and the like" (#311–8).

I had never thought of New York as vulnerable to earthquakes, and certainly nothing on the scale of severe destruction has happened there as yet. But Peterson pointed out to me that certain events in the 1930s at least suggested that Cayce may have been clairvoyantly perceiving vulnerable conditions beneath the surface.

"Approximately twenty-five miles west and northwest of New York City is the Ramapo Fault. The most significant earthquakes in this area occurred in 1737 and 1884, and they were large enough to cause limited damage to brick buildings in the area. More recently, between 1974 and 1983, sixty-one earthquakes were noted, the largest being only 3.0, however. But of special interest is a series of events on August 23, 1938. Multiple earthquakes occurred that day within a four-hour period. The largest was 4.0 and produced only insignificant damage. However, this quite uncommon activity was just a few years after Cayce's prediction had called attention to the potential vulnerability of New York."

These two points of corroboration were worth noting, but they fell short of a dramatic confirmation of a cataclysmic prophecy. The question remained in my mind, "Why haven't we yet seen some of the more catastrophic changes Cayce so vividly envisioned?" Peterson answered that for him the right *interpretation* of these millennium predictions requires a precise examination of the differences that can be found among Cayce's pronouncements.

"The readings contain conflicting predictions, and they fall into three groups." That was news to me. I had looked at all the predictions in chronological order, but had never identified specific categories in those prophecies. As Peterson explained his discovery of a pattern in these seventeen readings, I began to see them in a new way. In essence, his discovery was that three sets of earth change predictions exist in the Cayce files:

1. changes targeted for the year 1936
2. catastrophic changes
3. slow, gradual changes

These distinct sets of prophecies paint somewhat different images, and may even have come from three different sources within Cayce—just as a radio could tune in to three different stations playing three distinct types of music. As I would soon learn, Peterson had come to believe that the first two of these sets were, in fact, considerably less reliable than the latter one. But first, let's go back and revisit the millennium prophecies that were summarized in Chapter 2. In that chapter they were presented chronologically—that is, in the order in which Cayce gave them. However, this time let's look at Peterson's observations and the insights they provide about the earth change prophecies.

Predictions for 1936

When we looked at the Cayce prophecies as a whole, one pattern that stood out first for Peterson was the frequency of predictions targeting 1936. Fully a third of the predictions fit this category; and, in fact, most of the prophecies that have *any* specific date attached to them are for this one year. These readings were given between February 1932 and January 1936.

Not all of them speak of worldwide catastrophic change. They address a wide variety of geological, political, and spiritual issues. Unfortunately, at least taken at face value, most or all of these predictions didn't materialize. In fact, Peterson's check of the geological records for 1936 showed that it was somewhat below normal for seismic activity.

In some instances, Cayce seems to have adjusted his view of the timing of changes first predicted for 1936. For example, in January 1936 he gave a reading that backed off of earlier prophecies about earthquakes in San Francisco in 1936. Also, in regard to a shift in the rotational axis of the earth, Cayce's initial prophecies were for this tremendous change to happen in 1936, but later he recalibrated his timetable and targeted likely dates right at the turn of the millennium—1998 or 2001.

As Peterson and I examined the seven prophecy readings that dealt primarily with 1936, we saw that Cayce seemed to have viewed this particular year as some kind of watershed in modern history. For example, using the word "catastrophe" in reference to international relations rather than earthquakes, Cayce predicted in February 1932: "This had best be cast after the great catastrophe that's coming to the world in '36, in the form of the breaking up of many *powers* that now exist as factors in world affairs. . . . With the breaking up in '36 will be the *changes* that will make different *maps* of the world" (#3976–10). While I remembered Peterson's comment that geological records show 1936 as a slow year, I couldn't help but remember, too, that 1936 *was* a very significant turning point for many political events as the world moved closer to war.

Even if we recognize Cayce's accuracy for geopolitical prophecy regarding 1936, we're still left to conclude that he was flat wrong on the earth changes. The reasons for those failed predictions may be complex, and in Chapter 8 we'll look at possible explanations *and* their implications for the millennium.

Perhaps the most frightening of the 1936 predictions that didn't come true—although later restated by Cayce for the turn of the millennium—was a shift of the rotational axis. I wanted Peterson to give me an opinion about this extraordinary idea.

First he reminded me that "pole shift" can mean one of two things: (1) a magnetic pole reversal and (2) a rotational pole reversal. As I remembered from earth science class long ago, the magnetic and rotational poles of the earth are actually two different things—physically separate, located several hundred miles apart. Because of this, the north arrow on a compass doesn't point toward true north, but toward the magnetic north pole.

Many magnetic pole reversals have happened in the past, averaging roughly one every million years. However, Peterson pointed out, in the last four to five million years, the average has increased, and a shift is occurring approximately every 300,000 years. Interestingly, the last shift was about 700,000 years ago, meaning that we are now "overdue" for one.

If a magnetic reversal were to occur tomorrow, what could we expect? Some evidence supports the theory that not much would, in fact, happen. A volcanic rock unit in Arizona, formed during one of the more recent magnetic reversals, recorded the direction of the magnetic poles by the alignment of certain minerals. These directions can be measured, and they indicate that the reversal was a process that took many years—actually, several hundred years was required for the 180 degree shift of the magnetic pole. Because of this and because of the weak nature of the magnetic field, this type of pole shift is not thought to be capable of producing major earth changes. It might act as a minor trigger for some changes that are already set to occur, but we would not expect this type of shift to produce the major earth changes that are included in Cayce's millennium prophecies.

The other type of pole shift—a rotational one—would, however, produce extraordinary changes, almost unimaginably catastrophic ones. Peterson stated unequivocally that within the science of geology, there is *no solid evidence that a rotational pole shift has **ever** happened*. We do know that a great amount of energy is associated with the rotation of the planet. Because of this, it would take a tremendous amount of energy to disturb the present state of equilibrium. Perhaps only another astral body passing very near the earth or actually colliding could do something like this. Cayce never spoke in such terms, so it remains a mystery what he saw as triggering such an unprecedented earth change. Peterson's analysis seemed so convincing that I was left to conclude that this was one Cayce prophecy that might best be understood in a symbolic or metaphorical way. It seems very likely that by the turn of the millennium humanity will be ready for a new "compass point," a new sense of direction.

The Catastrophic Prophecies

A second category of earth change readings describes worldwide cataclysms. They target dates after 1936, or in some cases they are vague about timing. Many of the dramatic prophecies outlined in Chapter 2 are in this category. What's more, the ultimate earth change—a shift in the rotational axis of the earth—is also in this set of predictions, having been reprophesied for the beginning of the new century.

These catastrophic predictions are the millennium prophecies by which Edgar Cayce's name is known to millions. They are the headline grabbers. In fact, some of them sound so dire that it's hard to imagine civilization as we know it continuing if they come to pass.

Peterson, however, had a new angle on this set of catastrophic predictions; there was something unusual about some of them: a tag line at the end. Four words—"I, Halaliel, have spoken"—at the conclusion of readings such as 3976–15 suggest something out of the ordinary. I was amazed that I had never noticed this. I felt like the oblivious constable in an Arthur Conan Doyle short story, with Peterson in the role of Sherlock Holmes pointing out a clue that changed the shape of the mystery. "I, Halaliel, have spoken." What did that mean?

A quick check of Cayce's personal history was revealing. For a fourteen-month period—from October 1933 to January 1935—there were occasions on which another spiritual being apparently tried to use the entranced Cayce's body as a mouthpiece. That being identified itself as Halaliel. This was in sharp contrast to the normal way in which Cayce's mind worked to give a reading—i.e., putting aside his waking conscious self and allowing *his own* superconscious mind to provide the information. While it was still just a very small percentage of the readings during these fourteen months, nevertheless it forced a very important decision point in Cayce's development as a visionary, clairvoyant and seer. Halaliel requested the opportunity to become more or less the permanent source of Cayce's readings, but wouldn't (or couldn't) do so unless the conscious Edgar Cayce was willing.

This created quite a controversy among Cayce's immediate helpers and supporters. Would it be a step forward to accept a being that claimed to be part of an invisible, spiritual hierarchy? Finally, the decision was made: no. Cayce ultimately rejected Halaliel as his source.

Writing later, Edgar's son, Hugh Lynn Cayce, remembered that a majority of the group voted to reject the guidance of Halaliel in favor of "a higher attunement with the ideas related to the Christ Consciousness." In later readings, Edgar Cayce and this group of supporters were commended for the stand they had taken.

But who was this figure Halaliel and why might his guidance be less than reliable? Some traditional, esoteric literature has suggested that he is the "Lord of Karma" among the angelic hierarchy—that is to say, a force that is instructive but which teaches through problems and difficulties. Maybe Halaliel represents a point of view on the future: the only way humanity will change is to learn lessons through adversity. This seems to match how a later Cayce reading describes Halaliel's identity: "a leader of the heavenly host . . . who has made the ways that have been heavy— but as the means for *understanding*" (254–83). One way to learn is the hard way. In fact, when we are stubbornly resistant to change, the painful lessons may be the *only* way to change and grow.

For anyone who has trouble accepting something as ethereal as angels of the spiritual hierarchy, there's a more psychological way of looking at the possible source of this second category of prophecies. Within Cayce's unconscious mind itself there may have been a pessimistic view of the future. It could see that humanity desperately needs a new way of living on planet earth, but saw that transition coming only as a hard-earned lesson from destruction and hardship. "Halaliel" then becomes a way of labeling a state of consciousness or frame of mind within Cayce.

Another interpretation sees Halaliel as an archetype of the collective unconscious of human minds—not simply a part of Cayce's unconscious alone. In this view, Cayce wasn't so much tapping into an angel as he was a state of mind that any of us can reach. Halaliel represents a focus on *one way* that people grow and change: the path of hardship.

The point here isn't to debate the reality of angels. Instead, it's to recognize that one category of Cayce millennium prophecies may be coming from a distinct perspective. That point of view focuses on the painful, difficult way that change can come. Perhaps it will prove to be accurate. However, the third category intimates that a more gradual and graceful transition is equally possible.

The Gradual Change Readings

We must admit that much of what Cayce said about 1936 didn't take place (or has somehow been delayed). What's more, the *source* of most catastrophic predictions seems to have been intent on the harshest or most difficult scenario. So we're left to consider the third category of millennium prophecies about earth changes, and to try to gain a fresh interpretative insight—especially an insight that is hopeful. Seven readings by Cayce fall into this category, and they share three themes:

1. The *timing* of the earth changes cannot be foretold;
2. The changes will be gradual rather than catastrophic;
3. We, as spiritual beings, can have some effect on these events.

Together with Peterson I looked again at all seven, and it was easy to spot these recurrent themes. For example, Cayce was asked in 1932 to comment on disastrous changes that might come soon. Using biblical language he responded, "The hour ye know not, and the time ye know not." He went on to say that it would be more a matter of a spiritual awakening than a material disaster that was unfolding that year.

Another earth change reading in this category was given to a real estate agent in late 1932. Two previous readings for this same man described cataclysmic changes for 1936. But this one—number 311-10—had a different tone and orientation. When queried specifically about earth changes for Alabama (which Cayce had previously predicted), he now clarified this to be *gradual* rather than sudden alteration.

But even more significantly, this reading boldly asserts that much of what is to come is still fluid and is at least partially shaped by human attitudes and behaviors. "[It] may depend upon much that deals with the metaphysical. . . . There are those conditions that in the activity of individuals, in line of thought and endeavor, keep oft many a city and many a land intact through their application of the spiritual laws" (#311-10).

Yet another example of this gradual scenario is a reading from 1934 for an accountant who was familiar with the earth change predictions and wanted more details. He asked for a description of the outline of the Pacific coast after the catastrophes. But Cayce responded that it was dependent upon individuals or groups who might keep a spiritual attitude in respect to the needs of the times. Then he added, as if to say that even gradual changes are still leading up to something big: "That some are *due* and *will* occur is *written* as it were, but—as we find—as to specific date or time in the present this may not be given" (#270–32).

A final illustration of the gradual scenario is from 1939. Cayce was asked if Atlantis would rise again as we moved into the Aquarian Age. The questioner, a forty-one-year-old woman, wanted to know the exact date and if this would cause a sudden catastrophe. Cayce responded that, in fact, changes were coming and that by 1998 we would have seen many of them. But then he adds significantly: "This is a gradual, not a cataclysmic, activity in the experience of the earth in this period" (#1602–3).

By Peterson's own admission, "These readings forced me to change my interpretation of earth changes. They all seem to agree that the future will bring gradual, not catastrophic changes. And, if Cayce is correct and we can influence the future, their timing isn't predetermined."

As we talked about this further, he went on to share with me one concern that he has about this line of reasoning. It contains the potential for becoming rather unscientific, for assuming a little bit too much about humanity's control over the planet. On the one hand, Peterson is aware of supportive parapsychological research in psychokinesis (i.e., mind over matter) which lends some credence to the notion that human thought (especially *mass* thought) could have a physical impact. But at the same time, he cautioned me about overreaching, reminding me of a point he had made before, "Ultimately, the reason Mother Earth moves is to cleanse herself and recycle her materials."

That line of reasoning made a lot of sense to me, while not losing sight of the remarkable parallel prophecies of earth changes found in Cayce's readings and so many other traditions. The trick is to integrate the best of modern science with the best of clairvoyant warnings. Ultimately, we need to work on making a healthy relationship with the earth, plan prudently, and be ready to cooperate if earth changes happen.

A Geologist's Conclusions

What then is the bottom line for this professional geologist who has worked diligently to compare the knowledge base of his profession with the clairvoyant material of Cayce, whom he respects?

First, he has found many similarities, including troubled, vulnerable lands on the west coast of America and relatively safe lands in the northerly midwest region. However, there are differences, too. The science of geology does *not* support the possibility of the submergence of the west coast of America, as was indicated in Cayce's 1936 dream. In geological terms it is virtually impossible for the large area that includes the Sierra Nevada, the Rocky Mountains, and the Colorado Plateau to sink thousands of feet in a short time. These areas have been rising slowly for many millions of years, and for them to sink thousands of feet in several years is highly unlikely.

So what can we expect just ahead? If the key to the future lies in the events of the past, we can expect more earthquakes and volcanic eruptions in the areas in which they have already occurred. It's likely that one or more major earthquakes will shake California. The same holds true for other regions we now recognize as earthquake vulnerable. Time may eventually show a significant increase in such activity in the decades just ahead, beyond the statistical probabilities that geology has formulated. For now, all we can do is wait—and be prepared.

For Peterson the Cayce millennium prophecies that indicate a gradual transformation are more convincing than those that suggest widespread catastrophe in the immediate future. No doubt that scenario also makes it easier to envision how we could make positive transformations culturally and socially as we move into the new millennium. Worldwide devastation is hardly the formula for a creative uplifting of civilization.

Finally, turning from geologist to philosopher, Peterson concluded his remarks to me with these words, "Preparing for the future may be very important, but it's equally important to live our lives to the fullest *now*. If we do the best we know to do today, tomorrow will take care of itself."

Chapter 6

ANCIENT AND MODERN PROPHECIES OF THE MILLENNIUM

Edgar Cayce was not alone in prophesying about the coming millennium. Psychics and seers of other times and cultures came before him to make similar prophecies, although we have no reason to suspect that the waking Cayce ever knew of them. The correspondences among these independent sources are compelling. It is not enough evidence to claim any sort of "proof," because who can ever prove the future? But it does suggest that we should explore seriously these visions of the future.

Many ancient and modern sources echo the same themes about what the millennium will bring. This chapter samples a variety of prophetic traditions and modern-day visionaries, whose predictions are close parallels to the ones given by Cayce. The prophecies mentioned in this chapter come from Nostradamus, native American people (i.e., Mayans, Aztecs, and Hopis), the visions of near-death experiences, and two contemporary visionaries.

Nostradamus

The psychic most often compared to Cayce was the Frenchman Michel de Notredame—better known by the Latinized form of the name which he adopted upon university graduation, Nostradamus. Born in 1503, Nostradamus, like Edgar Cayce, was deeply committed to compassionate service and healing in his adult career. Whereas Cayce was relatively unschooled and approached healing as a clairvoyant diagnostician, Nostradamus was a trained physician. He gained some notoriety for his skills helping victims of the plague to regain health.

But it was not his medical skill that made him famous throughout Europe. After twenty years of medical practice, in 1550 he published the first of his books that combined useful daily knowledge with predictive insights largely based on astrology. These almanaclike volumes appeared annually for sixteen years. During this second phase of his professional career, he also published a book of home remedies (again, like Cayce, whose own home remedy suggestions have been published in several forms).

By far the most famous of Nostradamus' publications is a collection of visionary poems that first appeared between 1555 and 1558 and have stayed in print continuously for over four hundred years! Entitled *Centuries*, they were published as a series of books, each with one hundred quatrains, hence the title. However, some people have assumed that these collections of prophetic poems were titled so as to imply that they looked centuries into the future. Perhaps Nostradamus intended the ambiguity.

Like Cayce, Nostradamus was sought after in his own times. On two occasions the queen of France requested his predictive advice. Politicians and businessmen from all over Europe knew of his reputation and wrote for counsel before starting new enterprises. It was not merely in retrospect that these two men gained appreciation and notoriety.

In spite of their common reputation as prophets, there are many significant differences between Cayce and Nostradamus which make it hard to portray accurately the similarities in their visions of the twenty-first century. Perhaps most notably, the prophecies of Nostradamus are cloaked in astrological imagery, symbolism, and vague references which may be difficult for a person of our times ever to decipher. Although Cayce's language is no doubt difficult for most people to get used to, his predictions for the millennium are in many cases straightforward. Consider one example presented in Chapter 2: repeatedly Cayce said that the years 1958 to 1998 would be the four decades in which extraordinary planetary transformation would begin. The dates are clear and unambiguous. Not so with the quatrains of Nostradamus. They required interpretation from the time they were given, and that process continued after his death. In 1594, just twenty-eight years after Nostradamus' death, the first published interpretations appeared. Since then dozens of writers have attempted to unravel the meaning behind the enigmatic pronouncements of *Centuries*.

Some of the predictions in his quatrains seem unarguably accurate, particularly some that were fulfilled in his own century. For example, four years before the death of King Henry II in a jousting mishap, Nostradamus' predictive poem foreshadowed the sad event with details that proved to be valid. "The young Lion shall overcome the old one/ In a martial field by a single duel/ In a golden cage he shall put out his eye/ Two wounds from one, then he shall die a cruel death."

But unfortunately very few of the quatrains can be linked so specifically to historical events. Ambiguity and multiple possible meanings for various symbols make it very hard to say exactly what Nostradamus predicted, especially in regard to our upcoming millennium. Critics go so far as to say that trying to make sense of *Centuries* is like a Rorschach ink blot test; they allow interpreters to read into them almost anything they want. These skeptics argue that the imagery and astrological references are often so ambiguous—especially when one has nearly four hundred years of history through which to look for coincidental matches—that any claims of prophetic power beyond the sixteenth century itself are farfetched.

Others who analyze the evidence are more generous in their assessment, pointing out that Nostradamus seems to have had an uncanny ability to foresee air warfare and other aspects of modern life that could hardly have been dreamed of four hundred years ago. But there is an unmistakable *lack* of general agreement among the believers as to exactly what it was that Nostradamus predicted for our own era. Dozens of books in the last twenty years have offered a myriad of interpretations. On one count, however, all seem to agree. Researchers, translators, and scholars of the Nostradamus material all concur that he foresaw cataclysmic changes— even the destruction of the world. But the translations of his poetic imagery into calendar dates range from 1988 to nearly A.D. 3800. *Perhaps the best that can be said of the Nostradamus prophecies when compared to Cayce is that both predicted the likelihood of global destruction and transformation on a scale far beyond anything else in human history.*

Nostradamus and Cayce are not the only psychics who predicted the likelihood of dramatic earth changes. There have been literally dozens of psychics in the years since Cayce's death who have said similar things, often giving greater details and more specific dates than did Cayce or clearer imagery than Nostradamus ever offered. But in many instances those specific earth changes predictions have already proved to be incorrect. It is also hard to say to what degree the post-Cayce psychics were simply mimicking Cayce, whose influence on the profession of prognostication can hardly be overestimated. No, the case for the study of the Cayce earth changes readings is not significantly strengthened by psychics who followed him and who have basically reiterated his ideas on the topic. What we need are more sources of information that are likely to be independent of Cayce, and preferably predate his own work. The best such material comes from other cultural traditions.

Native American Prophecies

One especially noteworthy source of ancient prophecy about our own times comes from native societies of central and north America. The Mayan civilization is the most ancient in this part of the world, with the earliest archaeological evidence stretching back to 9000 B.C. in what is now coastal Belize. By 2500 B.C. the Mayans had established agricultural settlements.

The key to their success was an elaborate and highly sophisticated set of calendars that allowed for the precise timing of planting and harvesting. These calendars came from many generations of careful observations of the heavens, and they were actually several interlocking measurements of time, each with its own periodicity. The most significant of the Mayan calendars were the solar year of three hundred sixty days (divided into eighteen months of twenty days each) and the sacred almanac with two hundred sixty days (comprised of thirteen months of twenty days each). Once every fifty-two years a remarkable coincidence occurs as the same day comes up simultaneously on both calendars. This cycle was known as the Calendar Round, and formed the basis of some Indian prophecies—not only Mayan, but the other native cultures of Central and North America who were significantly influenced by the Mayans.

Especially significant to a comparison study of Cayce's millennium predictions is the four-hundred-year cycle the Mayans called "baktuns" and the series of thirteen consecutive baktuns called the Great Cycle—fifty-two hundred years. Our current Great Cycle is dated to conclude precisely on December 21, 2012. Mayan prophecy describes events surrounding this date as rather frightful, but mingled with signs of hope and breakthrough. To the generation that lives during that turning point will come "the day of withered fruit"; "the face of the sun will be extinguished because of the great tempest." But finally there will come blessings to renew humanity—"ornaments shall descend in heaps, and there will be good gifts for one and all." Although not exactly matching the dates that Cayce focused on, nevertheless the themes of painful transition and grace-filled conclusion are embedded in both prophetic sources.

By the tenth century A.D. the sophisticated and impressive centers of Mayan culture were abandoned, for reasons that are still relatively mysterious to scholars. Mayan civilization continued, but now at the modest level of village life, and other native civilizations rose in prominence (still highly influenced by many Mayan developments). The Aztecs and Toltecs were two such civilizations. Their culture hero and godlike figure Quetzalcoatl was a source of prophecies about changing times. His name roughly translates as "spirit of light," and he was revered as an ancient teacher of the people in the areas of mathematics, agriculture, theology and the arts.

Legend has it that Quetzalcoatl returned (that is, reincarnated) in a year now calculated to be about A.D. 947. There is considerable controversy concerning a date for his first incarnation, with some scholars of the opinion that there was no previous lifetime, that any earlier figure was mythological. Yet other writers and scholars assert that Quetzalcoatl was a historic character living sometime before Christ. For example, the renowned esoteric philosopher Manly Palmer Hall writes in *Twelve World Teachers:* "At some remote time a great initiate-king arose among the civilizations of Mexico and Central America. It is impossible at this late date to determine the period during which he lived, but it is safe to say that it was some centuries before the Christian Era." In *Voices of Earth and Sky*, anthropologist Vinson Brown describes the original Quetzalcoatl as the "Great Prophet of the period 200 B.C. to the beginning of A.D."

In this second life with his people, Quetzalcoatl foretold many important events and cycles of change to be experienced in the coming thousand years or so. His prophecies stated that within the ongoing fifth age there would be thirteen cycles, each comprised of fifty-two years. During these six hundred seventy-six years there would be decreasing consciousness and free will. Then would come nine cycles, once again of fifty-two years each, that would be characterized by darkness or hell.

Scholars use the year A.D. 843 as the starting point of all these cycles (that is, at the end of the classical period of Mayan culture). Quetzalcoatl's reincarnation would have come after two of these fifty-two-year cycles had already been accomplished, and some very interesting correspondence can be found to recorded history. If we look six hundred seventy-six years into the period (that is, the full thirteen cycles of diminishing consciousness and free will), we see that Cortez arrived in America in 1519 with his armies. And after a brief struggle he conquered and enslaved the people of this region.

The year 1935 marks the beginning of the final fifty-two-year cycle of darkness and hell. It is interesting to note that this date marks well the time when Hitler began moves to start World War II. The year 1987—that is, 1935 plus 52—was to be the final one in this last cycle of darkness. Then was to come the "great purification," reminiscent of Cayce's vision of global changes. This purification sounds dire: the equipoise of nature will be lost, the ocean tides shall obey no more, cities and mountains will collapse, leveled by great earthquakes. Although this kind of destruction did not occur in 1987, we are left to wonder if the timing has been delayed or if human choices may be altering what was once a likely future; indeed, according to a second prophecy, the intensity of suffering accompanying this purification would depend upon mankind's choices.

Despite the intensity of this purification process, the prophecies contain a hopeful view: a new era of cooperation, peace and plenty will be born. Quetzalcoatl promised to return "in the time of the great-great grandchildren of the white conquerors," initiating a new set of cycles, "a golden age of spiritual rebirth, planetary harmony, and for many the awakened consciousness of the Divine Life."

The Hopi Indians of North America provide another ancient tradition of prophecy that is remarkably parallel to the one given by Edgar Cayce. The immediate ancestors of the Hopi were the

"Ancient Ones"—the Anasazi—cliff dwellers whose history can be traced back to around 100 B.C. By the year A.D. 500 the Hopi had become a peace-loving, agricultural civilization that spread across large portions of what is now the southwest United States. The peak of the Hopi culture was approximately A.D. 1100, and they constructed impressive buildings at places such as modern-day Mesa Verde, Colorado, and Chaco Canyon, New Mexico.

The prophecies of the Hopi are said to have come from Massau'u, their spiritual teacher for the age. Ancient Hopi prophecies were handed down on stone tablets accompanied by an oral tradition of interpretation that was passed on by the elders of the community.

Certain of these prophecies concern events near the end of this current age in the Hopi framework of history. Some seem to have been fulfilled, including the coming of automobiles and telephones— "horseless chariots" that would roll along "black snakes" across the land, and "cobwebs" through which people would speak over great distances.

Among the prophecies is a petroglyph, or rock carving, that depicts the Hopi Life Plan Prophecy. In part, it shows two horizontal time lines, the top one representing our modern technological, materialistic society and the bottom line depicting the Hopi's own world of attunement to natural forces. Along the materialistic line are the figures of human beings with their heads detached from their bodies, an apt image for contemporary men and women whose intellectual self and feeling self are so often disassociated.

Also shown in this prophetic petroglyph are two vertical lines that connect the horizontal time lines. One of the connecting lines— symbolic of the opportunity for materialistic society to reconnect with the wisdom of the Hopi—is placed chronologically just before a pair of circles, which interpreters decipher to be the two World Wars. The second vertical connector comes after the images for these two great wars, at approximately the point in time in which we now exist. Thus, there is the opportunity, but not the certitude, for technological society to join with the wisdom of the ancient ones. If not, the Hopi Life Plan Prophecy depicts yet another period of great destruction. Beyond that point on the prophetic carving, the time line for materialistic society begins to fade out and disappear. The other horizontal time line, the one that is in harmony with the natural order, continues on.

Many Hopi prophecies have seemingly been fulfilled: trees everywhere will begin dying; people will build a house and throw it into the sky (perhaps the American space shuttle or the Russian space station); and dramatic changes will occur in the weather. With these signs confirmed, the Hopis believe that they can well expect the next stage in the prophecies, events to take place somewhere around the year 2000. The Great Day of Purification will be traumatic, but it will usher in the next age. Certain cataclysms like war, famine and earthquakes are predicted. However, their severity is something to be determined by humanity. The Hopi vision of the future includes the option for these catastrophes to be lessened, if humankind will work together in the proper spirit.

Near-Death Experiencers as Prophets

Another category of visionary is the near-death experiencer. Most research has focused on the remarkable similarities among accounts provided by those who were resuscitated after brief periods of clinical death. Since the publication of Dr. Raymond Moody's best-seller *Life After Life* and several other comparable books, certain common aspects of the near-death experience have become well known to millions: going down a tunnel, confronting a review of one's life, encountering a Being of Light.

But what has not been widely reported is that many near-death experiencers also have visions of the future during their brief moments in this extraordinary altered state of consciousness. Apparently, the near-death experience does not focus exclusively on one's own personal transition into the spiritual world. At least for some it also takes on global proportions, as one views current planetary conditions and catches glimpses of what may be ahead for humanity.

One researcher, Dr. Kenneth Ring of the University of Connecticut, has collected prophetic visionary accounts from several dozen near-death experiencers, which he reported in his 1984 book *Heading Toward Omega*. Ring distinguishes more common precognitive material—what he calls "personal flashforwards"—from a somewhat rarer kind of experience, the prophetic vision. This latter group concerns predictions with a planetary scope. What's more (and this is what makes Ring's research so intriguing) these prophetic visions are highly consistent from person to person. In his systematic assessment of prophetic visions of near-death experiencers, they seemed to be seeing the same sort of world about to emerge.

Before going into the details of these prophetic visions, it's interesting to note another characteristic that Ring discovered. Most of those who received prophetic visions had the clear sense that they had been shown or told far more than they were able to recall upon resuscitation from the near-death experience. Ring notes several factors that seem to stimulate recall in greater detail months or years later:

1. *Temporal proximity.* Some individuals claimed that within a few days of when an event was to occur, the knowledge of its occurrence would resurface.

2. *Spatial proximity.* For some individuals, being in a certain physical location seemed to trigger a more detailed recall of the prophetic visions they had been given during the near-death experience.

3. *Spontaneous recall.* For some visionary near-death experiences, details came back to mind several months or years later for no logical reason. Often their own interpretation of such spontaneous recall is that it was simply time for them to have access to the additional knowledge.

What, then, did these prophetic visionaries see in the course of their near-death experiences? Ring describes the elements of a model to which almost all of them conform. First, the visionary had a sense of being able to see the entirety of the earth's evolution and history. That is to say, any predictions about specific events were seen in a broader context. In spite of this panoramic view of time, the actual prophetic visions were much more narrow in scope and rarely extended beyond the beginning of the twenty-first century.

The visionaries share a view of the world in chaos as we move toward the end of the twentieth century: massive geophysical changes, huge disturbances in the weather and in food supplies. They see the economic system collapsing and the distinct possibility of nuclear war or accident. And yet, in spite of these dire images—perhaps even more severe than Cayce's millennium prophecies—the near-death visionaries have a collective sense of these changes being for the best. They are merely a very difficult transition into a much more healthy and spiritually enlivened culture in the twenty-first century.

While Ring's research on the one hand seems to corroborate the Cayce prophecies, there is still one highly significant *error* on the part of these visionaries. It concerns *timing*. As Ring himself states in his book published in 1984: "While agreeing that the date for these events are not fixed, most individuals feel that they are likely to take place during the 1980s." Most of the visionaries honed in on a date around 1988 or 1989, which surely must be judged now to have been wrong, unless we look at some of the prophecies symbolically and note the sudden and surprising downfall of communism in 1989 and the way that event shook and transformed the world.

Ring's book, written when there was still ample time for these prophecies to come true literally and within the predicted time frame, nevertheless tries to consider the visions from a number of angles. He is quite open to the possibility that the kinds of events described in these prophetic visions will come to pass, even by the end of the 1980s. But as a careful researcher and systematic thinker, Ring also notes that at an individual level these prophetic visionaries were enduring bodily pain associated with almost dying before their hospital resuscitation and transformation back to life. Their visions for the world reflect the same themes. Is it merely one's personal trauma being projected onto the grander canvas of international politics and world geology? Or, conversely, does a personal encounter with near death, resuscitation, and transformation make one more sensitive to receive those patterns and possibilities on a global scale?

Also noteworthy in Ring's book is a careful consideration of the workings of prediction and precognition. He looks at various models to explain how prophecy is even possible. Ring himself seems to favor a model that draws upon quantum physics and the idea that subatomic processes exist in terms of probabilities. For example, suppose that three alternatives exist for how a certain event will turn out. Perhaps alternative A is seventy percent likely; alternative B, twenty percent; and alternative C, ten percent. Quantum mechanics suggests that until the event occurs and is observed, each alternative outcome is associated with a wave function. When B is in fact the alternative observed, then the wave functions linked to choice A and C "collapse" just as B becomes a certainty.

However, another theory of reality suggests that A and C don't disappear. The so-called "Many Worlds Interpretation" or the "Theory of Alternative Futures" would say that A and C also "happen," even if we don't observe them from our perspective in the world where alternative B took place. As Ring notes, this notion is at face value rather outlandish and untestable. Nevertheless, it matches stories that Ring has heard from some of his near-death visionaries who have seen multiple lines of trajectory that lead toward the future.

Near the end of *Heading Toward Omega*, Ring makes use of this theory of alternative worlds to interpret the prophetic visions of his near-death studies. Ring suggests that his group may have connected with just one of a large set of alternative future scenarios.

Since they may not have suspected that other scenarios also existed, they had a sense of absolute certitude about what was actually only a probability. Perhaps, along some *other* trajectory that is *not* the one that we're on here in the late 1990s, those catastrophic events did play themselves out in an alternative world.

Admittedly it is a fanciful and untestable idea—untestable at least with any methods of investigation we currently understand. But the nature of reality is not limited by our three-dimensional logic. For example, so-called "imaginary numbers" don't "make sense" because they depend on the existence of some number multiplied by itself to make -1. Logic says there is no square root of -1. But what happens when we momentarily suspend that objection and theorize such a number, labeling it "i" for "imaginary"? That somewhat illogical approach ends up allowing us to solve many complex scientific and engineering problems having to do with the physical world. Maybe just as surely the alternative worlds theory helps us understand the apparent error in the prophetic visions of these near-death experiencers.

Visions of a Cultural Historian

Recognizing historical trends is one tool of the futurist, who can extrapolate to create a vision of what might happen. This principle can be applied to major cultural transformations in history. Recurrent themes appear in society's experiences of paradigm shift. Not only can we learn from these historical periods, but we can also formulate predictions of what may lie ahead for us.

One especially noteworthy cultural historian who has tried to do this is Dr. William Irvin Thompson, who has taught at MIT, York University and Syracuse University. In 1973 he founded the Lindisfarne Association, a contemplative educational community devoted to the study and realization of a new planetary culture. In a number of his books, particularly *Darkness and Scattered*

Light, Thompson examines the alternatives for the future, which he has inferred based on recurrent patterns of major historical change.

A summary of his ideas about these times of change fits nicely in our exploration of millennium prophecies. In many ways his theories closely parallel the concepts in the Cayce readings, although they are often much more explicit and detailed regarding a new millennial life-style. Like the Cayce readings, Thompson sees the latter portion of the twentieth century as a period for a paradigm shift at least as great as the Renaissance five hundred years ago. In his words, the change will be from civilization to planetization. Civilization is to be understood as a world order that focuses on material production and consumption. Planetization is a world order whose priorities are contemplation, consciousness and ecological balance. It is not that production and consumption will cease to be relevant issues in a planetized society, but rather we will have new priorities—or in Cayce terminology, new ideals.

The particularly difficult times of change, which Cayce foresaw beginning in the period from 1958 to 1998, are designated by Thompson as an initiation period for the earth. Using the three classic stages of initiation in mystery religions of the past, Thompson provides a framework for viewing both recent current events and predictions about our future. In other words, the ancient concept of spiritual initiation for an *individual* seeker may be acted out *collectively* by all of humanity. The traditional challenges and difficulties faced by the individual initiate may be analogous to the ones humanity will confront during these times of testing. Briefly, here are the three primary stages and, in Thompson's interpretation, the way in which we collectively may experience each phase:

1. *The illumination of one's darkness or shadow side.* The individual initiate might expect to face terrifying images from his own unconscious—the destructive, selfish potential within his own mind. Facing this inner demon can be not only frightening but

also discouraging. There are likely to arise feelings of doubt and unworthiness in seeing this shadow side of ourselves. This testing is felt most acutely by the initiate's ego.

When this state is applied to humanity as a whole, it is easy to see examples of the illumination of humanity's dark side, such as the wars in Viet Nam, Kuwait, and Bosnia, plus the ecological disasters caused by the misuse of technology. In Thompson's theory it is especially the elite of society (that is, the "ego" of a civilization) that experiences the humiliation of this first stage of initiation.

2. *Discovery of the edge of one's sanity.* For the individual initiate, this is the point at which he realizes that all the old definitions of reality no longer work. The old images of the ego no longer hold together. A breakdown in the sense of oneself and in the sense of reality results.

At a collective level, considerable evidence indicates that our society has entered this second stage of testing. The old systems and approaches upon which we used to depend no longer work. Many perplexing national problems seem to have no solution, and so many proposed solutions create even bigger problems while trying to solve the original difficulties. As one editorial in the *Washington Post* observed, no new ideas are around, and the old ones no longer hold things together like they used to.

3. *The defeat of the ego.* It is at this point in the individual initiation process that the seeker lets go. In that instant of openness and vulnerability, a new self-identity can be born. Our society has not yet reached this point. It may be years or decades away. As long as the leadership of a society convinces its people that the old ideas and identity might still be made to work again, the courage to surrender and let go will be wanting.

These three classic stages of initiation are the archetypes of transformation that historically have been known to only a few. The alchemy of changing consciousness is about to make a quantum leap—from the level of the single person to the level of humanity as a whole. As these three stages are enacted for the masses of the planet, Thompson predicts that they will affect different segments of society at different times. In his view, the changes will be felt first in the spiritual/religious community. This is not the group of religious leaders who hold stubbornly to the old paradigm. Rather, it is those who are genuinely open to a mystical revelation of what is being born in the world. Thompson cites Teilhard de Chardin as a good example.

The second segment is the artistic community. The new spiritual vision is given new life in art. Through art a great portion of humanity can sense the imaginative possibilities seen by the mystic.

For Thompson, the third segment of society to feel the impact of this new vision is science. Whether it is the architecture of people like Buckminster Fuller or mystic physicists like Fritjof Capra, the original vision of the attuned spiritual community finds expression for the masses in science. In fact, many modern-day physicists sound more like mystics than most ministers and priests of traditional Christianity.

The final segment of society to feel the change is the political faction. In effect, the political process is the last area to reflect transformation. It is the hardest to change, the most likely to depict our past rather than our future. In Thompson's view of change, cultural transformation is nearly complete by the time it reaches mainstream politics.

In Thompson's writings we find a description of various cultural forces at work to reshape the planet. One force is the emergent sense of world community. Even if we are not yet able to cooperate very effectively with other nations, the inescapable fact remains that our future and well-being are tied to that of other countries. The "planetization of the nations" is being felt first in its uncomfortable aspects—problems in one part of the world almost immediately create problems worldwide. But as a force for cultural change, this development could just as well nurture a sense of world fellowship. The days of a nation choosing isolationism are over. The planetization of the nations is ultimately a force for transformation that requires a choice between cooperation or suffering.

A second force at work upon our world is the decentralization of cities. In other words, there is a trend away from urbanization and a growing new respect for smaller communities as optimal places in which to live. As large urban centers of America (particularly the older cities of northeast America) decay, we shall be faced with hard choices about rebuilding them. Cultural forces at work point toward smaller and more manageable models for living instead of the urban centralization that has characterized the industrial age.

Thompson writes that the miniaturization of technology is a third force for transformation. At first glance it would seem that technology has been a part of the problem in the old paradigm. We might wonder how a product of technology could constitute a push toward developing a new set of assumptions for living. It is indeed ironic that the most remarkable of achievements of the old world order would create an impetus and an aid to a new life-style. However, this is exactly the effect that the miniaturization of technology has. Observe what has been made possible by computers or medical equipment so small they are portable. For example, on his or her laptop on a plane trip a business person can now have an information retrieval system as powerful as one that twenty years ago required a thousand times the space. When the technological tools for living become portable, the decentralization of population centers becomes possible. We no longer have to live in unwieldy urban centers to have access to the technological, medical and communications resources we need. The miniaturization of these tools for living open up new options in life-style.

A final, crucial force at work to change our world is the interiorization of consciousness. With this fourth force as well as the first one (that is, the planetization of nations) we find the most direct parallels between Cayce's and Thompson's millennium prophecies. As humanity begins to look for the source of the good life *within* rather than without, value systems begin to shift. A contemplative culture can emerge which finds new meaning in meditation, dream study, mythology and the arts.

In Thompson's view these four cultural forces work to create a new model for living, what he calls the meta-industrial village. The prefix "meta" means beyond, so the meta-industrial village is an evolutionary step beyond the life-style models of industrial life. The idea of village life may sound like a retrogressive step; it conjures up images of America in the days of George Washington: semirural communities with no electricity, no plumbing, no modern communications devices. But Thompson goes to great lengths to explain that this is not his vision at all. Although some proponents of "back to nature" would like to see us return to an eighteenth century way of life, he proposes a return to the village scale, but incorporating the technological breakthroughs of science. Communities of like-minded people—perhaps several hundred residents per village—can become models for new age living. Each such meta-industrial village would include:

1. *Energy self-sufficiency,* using a combination of replenishable energy sources, such as solar, wood and wind power.

2. *Agricultural self-sufficiency,* using organic or biodynamic methods for growing food that respect the delicate ecological balance.

3. *Cottage industries* for the production of salable goods. Such small-scale production could range from hand-crafted furniture to farm implements to microcomputers. The sale of products of the village's cottage industries would provide a source of income or a means of bartering items manufactured in other communities.

4. *Education of body, mind and spirit* for village members of all ages. Thompson beautifully describes this ideal in which "the entire village would be a contemplative educational community," with its basic way of life being "the adventure of consciousness. . . . Everyone living in the community would be involved in an experiential approach to education, from contemplative birth . . . to contemplative death."

The concept of the meta-industrial village is the end product of Thompson's theories and visions and an impressive contribution to speculations about the future. It seems to be quite consistent with the ideals and spirit of Cayce's perspective on a new millennium, but it is far more detailed and specific in its description than is any life-style model proposed in the Cayce prophecies. There appears to be no requirement in his vision that everyone live in such a village. We can well imagine that major cities will continue to exist into the twenty-first century. However, the quality of life and the security to be found in the meta-industrial village would likely attract many people—perhaps a majority—to this new model for living.

Visions of a Modern Mystic

Among the many teachers and psychically sensitive people who have written about a new millennium, David Spangler is a significant contributor. For several years he served as a formulator of educational development for the spiritual community Findhorn, in Scotland. Returning to America, he founded the Lorian Association and has been active in lecturing and writing about the emergent new world order. He describes his own method of receiving information on this theme as an attunement to both a universal consciousness and specific nonphysical beings in other dimensions of reality.

Among Spangler's various books, *Revelation: The Birth of a New Age* best expounds his ideas about these times of transition. An essential feature of that book is the notion that a new millennial consciousness is already here, but its current existence is simultaneous with that of the old world. The idea of two worlds may at first sound confusing, but if we look with sensitivity at what is going on within and without us, we may recognize that this is exactly the state of affairs in these changing times.

In Spangler's view, a new era is born first in the formative etheric energies of the planet—a level of subtle energy not yet a part of the established scientific worldview. A major shift has already occurred etherically. Nevertheless, the old world's momentum perpetuates its apparent reality and produces a seeming inertia to the change in etheric patterns. For centuries, old world assumptions have guided the creative dimensions of higher realities, which have in turn manifested as the physical world we have known. Even after the creative impulse is removed from these old etheric patterns, they continue to have their effect for some time. But they will necessarily play themselves out. They have within them the seeds of their own demise. An effective yet admittedly distasteful analogy is a chicken whose head has been severed, but who continues lifelike movement for a while.

When we take this concept a step further, it suggests to us a strategy for building a new planetary culture. Our forces should not be in conflict with the old. The old world will fail of itself—primarily, Spangler feels, because the creative input at the etheric level no longer exists. Our job is to be a part of the new world, to be attuned to a new consciousness that already exists and to learn to manifest its reality. Spangler puts it this way: "To know the new, one must be the new. To engage in conflict with the disintegrating patterns is to be at one with them, just as to use violence to stop violence is to defeat one's essential purpose. The old will separate itself naturally . . ." (*Revelation*, p. 170).

This philosophy about times of change is certainly found in the Cayce millennium prophecies, as well. To those who inquired about how to build a new world, he always responded this way: *focus on the positive.* In other words, both Cayce and Spangler point out that by keeping our attention directed toward whatever is helpful and hopeful, we play the most constructive role possible in allowing a new consciousness to emerge on earth.

Conclusions

One of the strongest and most reliable methods of investigation is to search for parallel statements and principles. Corroborative evidence is often the most dependable way to recognize reliable information. In this chapter we have examined half a dozen independent sources of prophetic wisdom, some dating back many centuries and some from creative thinkers of our own times. Although certain differences are to be found among these sources and the Cayce millennium prophecies, the large number of parallels is strikingly significant. This comparative approach makes even stronger the conclusion that the Cayce millennium prophecies are worthy of serious consideration.

But what is perhaps most impressive from this kind of parallel study is the sense that each of us who is living in these dramatic times of change has an important role to play. To some measure the future is still being shaped, and we have a say in making the new millennium what it will be. The final two chapters directly address this theme, starting with the idea that "earth changes" are as much an internal process as they are an external one.

Chapter 7

⌒

UNDERSTANDING THE INNER MILLENNIUM SHIFT

Have you ever dreamed of being in an earthquake? Or maybe you've had a nightmare of exploding volcanos or violent tidal waves. When these kinds of images appear in your dreams, they *might* be prophetic statements of impending natural disasters. But just as likely, they mean that you're going through your own *inner* upheavals. In fact, during times of personal stress, these kinds of images can be expected from the unconscious mind.

For most people the inner millennium shift has *already begun*. Earthquakes and other physical changes may or may not be following Cayce's prophetic timetable. But there's no disputing one fact: the inner millennium shift is moving ahead. The personal testing is already upon us.

Take a look at your own life. Some of your inner millennium shift challenges may be immediately obvious: health crises, career failures, stressful relationships. But inner changes are not always traumatic or catastrophic. In more subtle ways they can seep into our lives and in small, unobtrusive ways succeed in stretching us to our limits. Sometimes these inner changes are happening, but we're only marginally conscious of their importance; we occasionally go through a very significant personal test without being fully aware of what it's all about. But even when the inner millennium shift comes subtly in its expression, it almost always has a potent impact.

Of course, many of these kinds of problems have been going on throughout human history. What makes the times in which we live any different or special? Cayce's prophecy was that the late twentieth century and early twenty-first would be remarkable for the *pace* of demanding change and for its *pervasive* quality. Coupled with these two factors would be a simultaneous transformation of cultural values and crucial support systems. Just consider what happens when all these factors collide.

For example, it's one thing to go through a career failure, but at the same time still know what you believe in and where your values lie. People have been going through that sort of personal crisis for centuries. But it's quite another sort of challenge to lose your job and also live in a society that seems to have lost its rudder and forgotten what it believes in.

In a similar way, people throughout history have had painful, debilitating health problems, especially in old age. But usually there were community support systems to help. In our modern world, illness often brings with it a sense of alienation. For example, as the elderly become sick, they're often removed from familiar society and placed in isolated living conditions.

Other characteristics of the inner millennium shift are worth considering. As we see more and more of the features of these challenges, we're more likely to recognize these inner tests for what they are. Being able to name them and recognize their meaning is powerful medicine. Let's look carefully at a few of them.

One aspect of the inner millennium shift with which many people are struggling is a sense of *frustration*. Often that feeling is linked to a failure to connect with any sense of purpose in life. Nowadays vast numbers of people feel a lack of purpose. Virtually no one is immune. Even the person with a strong spiritual philosophy can nevertheless find himself in this situation. In fact, it's often the person who intellectually understands what these changing times are all about who *still* ends up feeling a frustrating lack of purpose and direction. In part this is because intellectual knowledge isn't enough. The changes happening in this millennium shift engage and challenge us at every aspect of ourselves: physical, emotional, intellectual, and spiritual.

In an effort to document how people of today are experiencing inner earth changes, I invited more than two hundred students of the Cayce material to submit written summaries of how the times of change were being experienced personally. Many of the accounts I received put an emphasis on the *pace* of life. For example, one woman's report said: "How am I currently experiencing the times of change? Very fast! Everything seems or feels very fast. A problem comes up fast, and the solution come up fast, too. Communications, relationships, health—I don't know how to put this into words!"

This person went on to describe that the critical role played by *balance* is moving from one unexpected spot to another. Properly approached this movement takes on the quality of a joyful dance: "Everything about these changing times for me is like walking, taking steps, always poised and flexible enough to put my next step down in a different place than I expected. The challenge is to stay in balance when a stepping stone is moved after I've already started to take the next step. Or perhaps the challenge is to be ready to jump to a different stone. It's not uncomfortable now, as it was at first. . . . It feels more like doing a dance and enjoying it."

For other people the essence of these times of change has been a test of desire and will. Most notably, our failures and disappointments force us to surrender our familiar sense of what's best. Inner earth changes often mean giving up willfulness. As one woman put it: "My world in these times of change has been completely shaken up over a period of a few years. It has been just like gigantic thunderstorms in most areas of my life. I have been going through a process of learning how to withdraw, lose, and give up the things I desire, whether I want to or not. Emotionally, it has not been easy. To adapt with sanity, I have to continue to flow through it and learn to trust in a higher power."

Another person focused his analysis on the need to be fluid and refrain from unnecessary battles—especially battles against inevitable change: "I experience tremendous changes in the workplace, economy, and society. It has been difficult to adjust initially, but now I am letting go and trying to flow with it. I am admitting that old structures, both in the workplace and in personal life, are not worth supporting in battle. In fact, the change will, as I accept it, help me to grow. It's an adjustment. But I know that to fight it is to lose."

Simply having knowledge doesn't make us immune from confusion. Possession of book learning doesn't necessarily mean that the ideas have been fully internalized. Yet, in spite of knowledge about the millennium prophecies, any of us can nevertheless slip into a frustrating lack of purpose. With a part of our minds we can be very objective and "on top of things," but with another side of ourselves we can directly experience pain and disorientation as the old ways die.

Each one of us must go through this death and rebirth process, for, to varying degrees, each one of us has "bought into" the traditional, mainstream world that is going through such difficult changes. And therefore, that aspect of ourselves invariably must experience the transition. This, in essence, is what inner millennium shift is all about. When we have overwhelming feelings of fatigue or a despairing lack of any sense of direction, it's all very natural; we are just passing through the test of transformation. We don't need to feel guilty for those days when we're caught up in our personal, inner millennium shift.

Not only do many of us feel a lack of energy as old patterns are dying, but frequently also a lack of enthusiasm. We may go through periods when the desire is just not there to do what we have long thought was good for us. This may surface as a dry spell in our prayer or meditation life. It may be a period of having no commitment to the nutrition that we know is best for us, or it may be a general lack of caring and enthusiasm for working on a problem relationship.

For other people a nagging sort of *anxiety* sets in when the inner millennium shift begins. In a society that is changing as fast as ours, what can we depend on? Not interest rates, not prices. Not our political leaders nor our physical environment. Next week there may be an earthquake in our backyards, or we may discover that our community's water supply is polluted with industrial waste. We can fall into worrying. "What will come next?" We can become numbed by all the changes. We can become frustrated to see the many people, institutions and conditions that were once so stable now appear so unreliable. In the midst of this, who can really plan for the future? And without a future to work toward, how can one have a sense of purposefulness in life?

That's a dismal way of thinking, but lots of people follow that line of reasoning. The sense of pessimism is strong. It's a widely held belief that the lives of our children will not be as good as our own have been, at least in terms of a material standard of living. And that reflects a radical shift in the attitudes and spirit of the American people over the last generation. One way of interpreting such an alteration is to look at it in terms of the inner millennium shift. Those changes are undermining the morale of the nation— and it's probably not just in America. People in great numbers are anxious, pessimistic and unenthusiastic about their own lives and about the future.

But there are certainly options available to us. There are other ways of responding to the inner millennium shift. Admittedly the challenge sometimes seems daunting. Events and conditions appear to shift so rapidly that it's hard to find any steady points of reference. Confusion, fatigue, and anxiety are natural—sometimes even the norm. Virtually no one is going to be immune from these symptoms. They come from living in a world that is being fundamentally altered.

However, feelings of despair and pessimism need not become a way of life or a permanent state of consciousness. Cayce's prophetic visions contain a purposeful, hopeful impression of the outcome of these changes. The "testing" really does have a reason.

Of course, the word "test" has negative connotations for most of us. Even if you did well in school, there's bound to be a measure of anxiety or resentment attached to the word. Perhaps we can find a new feeling to associate with it—one that reminds us of strength and accomplishment that can come with meeting a trial and successfully proving oneself.

Cayce suggested that each of us is being tested by the Creative Forces of the universe. This has always gone on; human life has always contained challenges through which the depths and beauty of the human spirit can emerge. Something is special, though, about these times in which we live right now. The test is one with higher stakes—not so much for us personally, but for humanity as a whole and for the planet itself. And in this case, the "testing" is not so much like an exam that we might fail and then be expelled from school. Instead, it's a kind of testing that comes for our own benefit—to push us into being something better. It will force us to make changes in ourselves, changes that are likely to make us more capable of living in a different sort of social world and even physical world.

Cayce's visions of the future describe a very different kind of world than the one we're familiar with. The distinctions aren't simply the positions of coastlines or mountain ranges. We're passing through a period of personal and collective testing because it's preparing us to live in a planetary culture that operates by a new set of rules and assumptions. We can see the first hints of this fact already. We're discovering that we truly *are* a world community. The ancient concept of national boundaries is becoming very elusive. Examples quickly come to mind. We're inseparably linked economically. We share an atmosphere and a set of interconnected oceans. We're linked electronically around the globe with a kind of technological nervous system for the human family. The evidence continues on and on, leading to one inescapable conclusion: We live in times when the world is being turned upside down. It really *is* a whole new ball game, and we'd better be ready to play by a new set of rules, assumptions and principles.

Cayce's contemporary Carl Jung had a similar notion. (The two were born just two years apart, though they did their work without direct knowledge of each other.) Jung coined the term "modern man" to refer to just the sort of woman or man who was prepared to move beyond the traditional world. Such an individual was ready to be a citizen of just the sort of world that we are now thrust into—whether *we* are ready for it or not. Writing in the 1930s, Jung describes in his book *Modern Man in Search of a Soul* such a courageous step. But it's one that he sees as more or less optional, chosen by relatively few. As we near the end of the twentieth century, it now seems that *all* of us must be ready for what Jung envisioned decades ago:

> Only the man who is modern in our meaning of the term really lives in the present; he alone has a present-day consciousness, and he alone finds that the ways of life which correspond to earlier levels pall upon him. The values and strivings of those past worlds no longer interest him. . . . Thus he has . . . estranged himself from the mass of men who live entirely within the bounds of tradition. Indeed, he is completely modern only when he has come to the very edge of the world, leaving behind him all that has been discarded and outgrown, and acknowledging that he stands before a void out of which all things may grow.

With the inner millennium shift, we're each being challenged to become just such "modern women and men." Cayce's vision about the very times in which we are now living emphasizes one basic principle: For each of us there already is—or soon will be—a test that gives us the opportunity to prepare ourselves for the millennium, for the new root race (as it was described in Chapter 3). "You expect a new root race. What are you doing to prepare for it?" (#470–35).

For many of us that preparatory challenge is found in some part of our lives where we are especially being made to feel uncomfortable, to feel pinched. It may be in a particular kind of interpersonal relationship. For some it may lie in finances. For others, it will be a desire pattern of body or mind that needs to be curtailed.

But whatever it is, we have one thing in common during this test to prepare us for living in the twenty-first century. Pressure is being put on something we have directly placed between ourselves and God. The test is a challenging opportunity to *change our relationship to God* by altering something in ourselves—be it a worry, desire, attachment, fear or anything else.

In many cases the requirement of the preparatory test is merely to *move* something, not necessarily remove it, from our lives. For example, if our test is in terms of a preoccupation about money, then the challenge is to assign money a lower priority in our lives and put God first. Having passed through the test, we might still use money in our daily affairs, but its importance in our lives would have changed.

In another case, the test might be in a relationship with a person to whom we are overly attached. Perhaps what is required is a change of priorities, not necessarily removing that person totally from our presence. Again, the test is to discover how to put God first in our lives. If we can do that, then we are much more likely to be psychologically and spiritually comfortable with the values of an emerging new world that Cayce foresaw. However, the work that is required of us in order to pass through such a test—the alterations we have to make—will indeed feel like upheavals and earth changes inside of us.

The Dynamic Quality of God

In order to cope with and understand the inner millennium shift, we need a clearer notion of how God works in the material realm. So many spiritual teachers and writers of sacred literature have spoken of the timeless, eternal, unchanging quality of God. In these times when outer conditions change so rapidly, they might counsel us to put our trust in the one thing that *never changes:* God's perfect spirit and love for us.

Undoubtedly, great comfort may be found in experiencing first-hand this characteristic of the Divine. However, if our knowledge of God never grows beyond that experience, it implies that the world of change around us has nothing to do with God. Simply understanding God to be the steady point of reference in the midst of whirlwind change actually misses the full picture of our Creator.

The nature of God is paradoxical. From the reference point of human consciousness, God is best understood as a two-sided coin or as the two poles of a bar magnet. Certainly, God is a steady, reliable consciousness of love that never wavers. However, God is *also* the god of unfoldment and of evolution. God is creativity and hence the change that accompanies any creation.

Dealing with this paradox is a crucial challenge for our times. As with most polarities or paradoxes, we might be tempted to embrace one side of the truth and exclude the other side. A good example of this is in religious fundamentalism (not just Christian fundamentalism). It's no secret that religious fundamentalism has been on the rise throughout these final decades of the old millennium.

Fundamentalists have a strict notion of God's nature; it's basically a static one. Of course, they do admit that God may cause *some* changes now and then; for example, in the Old Testament we find stories of how God causes the destruction of cities and people because spiritual laws are not being obeyed. But for the fundamentalist of any religious persuasion, God is to be worshipped mainly because of one reason: the unchanging, timeless reality of divine existence and spiritual laws.

It's just as possible to embrace the other side of the coin. But inherent problems exist if we exclusively adopt the opposite end of the scale and claim that God is only the God of creation and evolution. Now things get slippery and vague. What happens if we say that each generation must discover its own spiritual realities? It eliminates any sense of continuity, and we can fall into the mire of relativism. Suddenly we have no point of reference. Everyone is doing his or her own thing. We can easily muddle the distinction between genuinely creative acts and self-indulgent habits. Claiming that everything is always changing leaves us with no awareness of where we are going—simply because there is nothing against which we can measure ourselves.

No, the answer lies at neither end of the polarity. Like all other polar tensions, the answer is the middle way—the midpoint of the continuum. Like all paradoxes, we're forced to find a third truth, one that can include both of the other two.

This leads us to one of Cayce's most important millennium prophecies. In the years just ahead we will come to a new understanding of God and the Creative Forces that shape the universe. What will this new understanding look like? On the one hand, Cayce predicts that we will come to see more clearly than ever that God's influence is dynamic and transformative. When we feel tests and pressures to change, it's the work of our Creator that we experience. But at the same time we'll come to a deep understanding of how God brings influences that are constant, reliable points of reference.

It's to be a balancing trick for us. We need to be guided by the unchanging truth of spiritual law *and* simultaneously accept the divine nudges to evolve and grow into something more than we have been.

Higher Dimensional Life

For those who find abstract analogies or models to be helpful tools for understanding, here is one that may be especially useful. It illustrates what's going on when we're "stretched" by the force of change in our lives. The essence of this analogy was proposed by a Tibetan Buddhist teacher, Lama Anagarika Govinda, in his book *Creative Meditation and Multi-Dimensional Consciousness.* And even if such abstractions "aren't your cup of tea," give this one a try. You may still find that these images stimulate an intuition about how the times of testing are potentially expanding our consciousness.

Let's playfully create a picture of what the inner millennium shift may do to human consciousness. Imagine that your self-awareness is two-dimensional. Suppose, for example, that it's just the surface area of a square drawn on a tabletop. You have length and width—but not height, because you are just a surface.

Now, take the analogy one step further as you imagine being this square living on a tabletop. Suppose you are entering times of change. You are experiencing challenges that test you and try to push you to grow into a higher dimensional being.

In fact, that's just what living in modern times feels like. We're being nudged into a higher dimensional awareness. In Lama Govinda's analogy we, as two-dimensional squares, are being pushed to become something more: three-dimensional cubes.

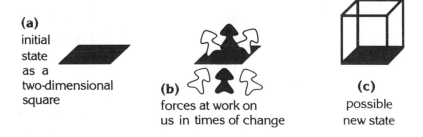

(a) initial state as a two-dimensional square

(b) forces at work on us in times of change

(c) possible new state

What do we experience as we're pushed through this transitional point between the old and the new? We feel like we're being stretched, and it comes quite naturally for us to be afraid. But afraid of what? Basically it's the fear of our own destruction. The square worries that in becoming a three-dimensional cube its original "squareness" will be destroyed. In other words, we worry that in these times of change—inner and outer—our old identities will be destroyed.

Fear is a big topic for our times, so let's look at it more carefully here in the analogy. The fear is reasonable under only one condition: the impact of forces of change *in the familiar dimensions we already inhabit.* In Govinda's imaginative analogy, the square should be afraid only of the forces that try to alter its length and width. For example, certain forces might try to change it into a triangle, pentagon or some other two-dimensional figure.

But certain *other* forces of change do *not* threaten the square's identity. The forces of change that challenge the square to be transformed into a cube aren't threatening in the same way. Those forces that want to stretch the square into a three-dimensional cube aren't concerned with altering the "squareness." *They want to build upon what's already there!* In exactly the same way, Cayce's millennium prophecies invite us to see the new world that must be built upon what is already here. That's just as surely true of the new self in each one of us that is trying to be born. It's to be a lifting and transformation of what we already are.

So what kinds of forces are we dealing with most often in these times of change? The first type or the second? The ones that try to undermine who we know ourselves to be *or* the ones that try to stretch us by building on what we already are? The inner millennium shift is most often about the second kind. The familiar, traditional ways of life exist in the two dimensions of our "squareness." Those forces are usually content to keep going on in just the ways they have been. The forces of change come from a higher dimension, trying to transform us into a richer awareness of life. And therefore, more often than not, our fears about self-destruction in these challenging times are based on a misunderstanding of what's going on.

The analogy demonstrates beautifully why fear is unfounded. Who we've known ourselves to be isn't on the verge of destruction. Rather it's something to be built upon. The square is not eliminated as the cube is created. Look carefully at the cube in the illustration and see that the original square is still there. But what has happened to it? *Its relative importance has been redefined.* Previously it was the "whole show," and now it has become only a part of a greater whole. This is what we can expect as the inner millennium shift does its work on us. Our current identity isn't to be destroyed, but instead put into a new perspective. We are being tested to become more than what we are now. The old will be given a new place. Many of our current likes and dislikes, many of our current habit patterns of living, must be seen in a new perspective. Their relative importance in our lives must be redefined.

A Model for Understanding Inner Changes

One way to better understand the inner millennium shift is to borrow a concept from gestalt psychology, a type of perceptual psychology formulated in Germany. Its essence is the question of how we perceive the world. Consciousness itself is largely a perceptual matter. Your awareness is determined mainly by what you "see," both in an outward physical way and in your subjective impressions of the inner world. When these pieces of outer and inner experience are put together, they create the "gestalt" that is functional for you in the moment.

Gestalt psychology questions the mechanism within us that makes certain objects or patterns in an overall field of view stand out, whereas other objects or patterns remain as background. The synthesis of these elements—some foreground and some background—creates the overall perception or experience we have. The classic example is the visual paradox which most of us have encountered:

What do you see? A white goblet or two darkened faces? Probably you see both, but not at the same time. In any specific moment of perception, certain items stand out as foreground and others recede as background. The "gestalt" under which we operate in our perceptions is merely a control system that selects certain things to perceive while others are generally ignored. If your gestalt defined white space to be insignificant in the drawing above, then you would see the two faces. However, another gestalt would also have been possible for you, one that would cause you to see the goblet.

Gestalts become ways of thinking or states of consciousness. Suppose as a teenager you were frequently lonely and never had dates, even though you wished you could. With the consciousness you had at that age, what kind of gestalt controlled your perceptions of life around you? For example, walking through a shopping center on a Saturday afternoon, what did you see? What emerged as foreground perceptions most likely were members of the opposite sex about your own age. Most else was not of interest to you and was little noticed. But suppose you are now forty years old, married with three children, and it is the Saturday afternoon before Christmas. You are in a shopping center trying to get last minute shopping done. What do you notice? What does your current consciousness—your present gestalt—select as foreground perceptions? Perhaps bargain-priced toys in store windows. Perhaps the clothes that other children you pass are wearing. You are a different person than you were as a teenager. Your consciousness has changed and, therefore, so have your patterns of perception.

This principle of a gestalt leads us to a related concept which will give us a key to inner millennium shift. That concept is the "paradigm." Simply stated, a paradigm is a set of assumptions that creates a mind-set for perceiving the outer world, or even for seeing oneself. It's much like a gestalt, although the term "paradigm" is used more frequently, in many disciplines.

Usually a paradigm refers to an agreed-upon set of assumptions which a group of scholars or even a whole society has adopted. However, this "agreement" is often passed on in an automatic or unconscious way. Within a given academic discipline, new students learn the old paradigm from their teachers and then years later teach it to additional new students.

For example, there is a paradigm within the domain of Egyptology. Those assumptions include a time frame that does not permit much in the way of civilization to have occurred in Egypt before 3,000 B.C. With that mind-set each new archaeological discovery is viewed and categorized within the agreed-upon assumptions. The paradigm of modern Egyptology is made up of a handful of key assumptions. Rarely are those assumptions questioned. Anyone trained in this field professionally "joins the club" by ascribing to the mind-set of his or her colleagues.

Some latitude may be permitted within the group that shares a paradigm. There is occasionally room for creativity. But that creativity is to be directed toward the discovery of further assumptions which can be *added on* to the existing paradigm. However, within some groups—such as religious orders with their assumptions about God and the proper way to live—there may be no room at all for truly creative thinkers. The assumptions have been set; there is no room for more. The only "creative" work to be done within such groups is to discover new ways to match up the assumptions, to find new correlations. In other words, groups or fields of study with rigid paradigms are interested only in finding new ways to "prove" what they have already assumed is true.

Admittedly, a study of paradigms can become rather confusing. There are so many different varieties of paradigms, how does one know which are relevant to one's personal journey toward understanding? The problem is complex because our modern world is comprised of so many different fields of study. It was far easier in earlier times. There might have been only the religious and the political paradigms of the day. With only two—which rarely got in each other's way—life was more straightforward. The local priest would tell you about the religious assumptions concerning God and the afterlife. The king or his local representative would tell you about the political assumptions—who were the good guys and who were the bad guys, and whose orders to follow. Areas of study such as agriculture and science had to fall in line with religious and political paradigms of the day. People like Galileo rudely discovered this fact when they tried to assert new assumptions for science which contradicted the established norms.

But in our times around the turn of the millennium, things are a bit more hazy. It's hard to identify very clearly the prevailing mind-set for areas like religion and politics. And the set of assumptions for certain scientific disciplines, such as physics, has been changing quite rapidly. Nevertheless, there seems to be a common ground to the mind-sets of the various groups, disciplines and organizations of the mainstream culture. There are points of overlap and a few basic assumptions that the majority of people in Western culture hold in common. We can call this the "old world paradigm" to contrast it to a "new world paradigm" which characterizes Cayce's visions of the twenty-first century and beyond.

Before attempting to identify the specific items of the "old world paradigm," we should make it clear that not every person in Western culture ascribes to these assumptions. Some people already live fully under the "new world paradigm." Others of us shift back and forth. We have days or moments in which consciousness moves and we suddenly see life and ourselves through the eyeglasses of the new assumptions. But then we find ourselves slipping back into the familiar, old world view.

What, then, does this "old world" view of life look like? What are its assumptions? The list might well include assumptions like those below. They are certainly *not* what Cayce's millennium prophecies predict for the twenty-first century mind-set. But these ways of seeing life still hold powerful sway today:

1. *Humans aren't really part of nature.* Even though we may have descended from apelike ancestors, we are now apart from the natural world. It's not necessary to try to be one with the planet Earth because it is basically dead. We do things *to* the earth and nature not in cooperation *with* them.

2. *Supply is limited.* There is only so much energy and so much food. The universe is running down. Entropy controls not just the cosmos, but our own little microcosms as well. There is simply not enough for everybody.

3. *People are generally selfish or evil.* The essence of the human spirit is to get what you want. People cooperate only when it is likely to lead to some reward.

4. *Bigger is better.* Quantity determines value. The more people who buy a book or see a movie, the better it is. The more money a person or a company makes, the more successful they are.

5. *Things are real only if they can be physically measured.* Concepts such as thought energy, ESP, and healing vibrations are all merely delusions.

6. *There is only one truth,* and once we think we have it, it is our obligation to make sure others adopt it and the world is run by it.

These six assumptions aren't the only ones that might be on the list, but they're an effective sampling of the world view that is familiar to us. They create a mind-set for perceiving the outer world and ourselves. The assumptions create an interlocking matrix which is very resistant to being tampered with. However, it's just this paradigm that is under siege in today's world.

Where is the paradigm? It isn't locked in a bank vault somewhere to keep it safe. *It's within human minds*, within human consciousness. And the old world paradigm is being challenged by an emergent new set of assumptions—directly contradicting not just one or two of these six, but all of them.

Because the old world paradigm is within us, we feel the strains of it being challenged. Our own minds are the battleground. And this is one meaning of the inner millennium shift. The foundations of the old world view of life are being shaken and we feel it.

Alternatives for Handling Paradigm Shifts

History shows us that occasionally the assumptions by which humans view life can shift dramatically. The change from the Middle Ages to the Renaissance is a good example. During this transition period, which spanned more than one hundred years, some of the cornerstones of medieval thought were shaken. A world that was universally understood to be flat was discovered to be spherical. The Earth, believed to be at the center of the Solar System, was found to be only one of many planets traveling around the Sun. The Protestant Reformation transformed Christianity. There was a clear paradigm shift in Western culture.

Since the beginning of the Renaissance, there have certainly been major changes in our world and in human assumptions about reality. Breakthroughs in science and in the technology of warfare in particular have altered our life-styles and thoughts about the world in which we live. However, the transition in human awareness which Cayce and others foresee in the coming generation is the most dramatic paradigm shift since the fifteenth century. Once again, there is a possibility that nearly all the assumptions held by the vast majority of a society will be challenged and replaced.

It's not easy to live through a paradigm shift. An ancient Chinese curse is noteworthy. It is translated by some, "May you live in times of change," and by others as, "May you live in interesting times." Either way it resonates in our own era. It's difficult to live under such conditions because there are so many ways that people respond to changing assumptions and perceptions. Everyone seems to react differently to the uncertainty, and it's hard to know where people stand. Common understanding and belief make life simpler, and their lack can be frustrating. For example, someone living in 1500 might not have known if a new acquaintance was a "flat Earth man" or a "round Earth man." Or someone living in 1550 might have worried whether his neighbor was joining the new Reformation movement or remaining loyal to the traditional church. In our times we wonder how the person sitting next to us on the airplane will react if we talk about meditation or ecology. Or we hope that our relatives will understand if we quit a lucrative but demoralizing job in order to take work that creates personal joy.

The sense of community among people is easily threatened in times of paradigm shift. And added to this is the personal stress we feel—the inner millennium shift—as the old ways in us begin to die. This extraordinary mix of factors is what Cayce foresaw decades ago as he envisioned the turn of the millennium. It all produces an exciting, troublesome, anxious age.

And so, how are we to *respond* to times like these? There are two alternatives. We can try to hold on to the old paradigm, or we can embrace a new set of assumptions which is being born. Let's look first at some of the elaborate schemes that people sometimes use in trying to hold on to the old ways.

Holding On to the Old Paradigm

This option is the equivalent of "Let's go down with the ship." Some people are so determined to stay with what's familiar that they even contribute indirectly to their own demise. Of course, it probably doesn't look that way to them. For those who persist with the old mind-set, the adversity is merely a challenging test of their loyalty to the truth.

And so the people of our times who want to retain the six assumptions previously listed have a case to argue. They are defenders of a worldview that has, in many ways, served us well. Those half dozen assumptions—that familiar paradigm—has been a world view that has produced many fruits. Look at the progress of humanity in the past two centuries, they point out. They argue that there's no reason to believe that the same world view cannot continue to produce results. In fact, one definition of political conservatism is "applying the worldview and methods that have solved problems in the past to the new problems that face us today."

However, the difficulty with a conservative approach comes if there's an unwillingness to look at facts. The old world mind-set operates with a gestalt that makes anomalies (events or conditions that contradict one of the assumptions) seem like background, at best. *They don't see what others see.*

For those of us who have experienced contradictions of one or more of the old assumptions, it's very frustrating. Old paradigm thinkers refuse to see or admit what we know to be true. However, it may not be lying or conspiracy or deceit on the part of the people trying to hold on to the old assumptions. Perhaps they really cannot recognize something because for them it's only a part of the background. For them it's as if those anomalies don't exist.

Let's look at two modern examples. There are many instances in which a group of people seems to refuse to look at the evidence. Consider psychic ability. Although a majority of people may say that they believe there's something to ESP, this isn't the case among key decision makers, scholars, scientists and others in positions of intellectual authority. For this influential group, it's as if the strong scientific evidence for ESP doesn't exist. Generally they either refuse to admit that the reports of parapsychologists are true or they refuse to make the effort to look into these matters. Naturally it's frustrating for backers of parapsychology. More than thirty years of carefully controlled scientific research has been meticulously documented in *The Journal of Parapsychology* and *The Journal of the American Society for Psychical Research*. These researchers and their advocates believe that an understanding of ESP might help change people's attitudes about the human family. What's more, psychic sensitivity is a skill that Cayce foresaw as widespread in the twenty-first century.

However, we might wonder why so many intelligent individuals in our society so resistantly hang on to the old world assumption that there's nothing to telepathy (mind-to-mind communication) or psychokinesis (mind over matter). But consider how threatening such a shift in belief would be to some of the leading thinkers of our world. For example, most all of the previous findings of *psychological* research would become suspect, because telepathy (conscious or unconscious) might possibly have influenced the experimental subjects to do or say what the experimenter hoped. Decades of very expensive research would suddenly lose much or all of its reliability. Just think, too, what would happen to research methods in physics or chemistry if one had to account for the possible effects of psychokinesis. Here is a phenomenon that, if true, is so elusive that it cannot easily be shielded or measured. For many people, too much is at stake to readily shift assumptions and take an open-minded look at the findings of parapsychology.

Ecology provides us with a second good example of how some people try to resist a new way of looking at life, especially when that new way seems to threaten their own professional or personal investments. In the last three decades there's been considerable progress with the environment. And to a growing number of people there is clear evidence that we have polluted the oceans and air, perhaps to a point beyond repair. Furthermore, it seems increasingly clear that humans are very much a part of an ecological whole—when we do something to affect nature, then we've got to expect to get something of equal quality back in return. And yet that sort of assumption runs contrary to the mind-set that has created a heavily industrial world. It threatens a life-style based largely on plastic and mass-produced, interchangeable goods. The leaders of such industries, and the people who have become dependent upon them, are inclined not to see the anomaly. Their gestalt places in perceptual background the disturbing new evidence of what we are doing to our planet. They tenaciously hold on to the old paradigm.

Refusing to consider the evidence that might require a shift is the most simplistic response, but this is only one method by which people try to hold on to the old set of assumptions when the world is changing. A more subtle technique is trying to *patch up* the old system. It looks like an open-minded willingness to change, but in essence is not that at all. The steps for this approach go as follows: First, identify the assumption that seems to be disproved by an anomaly. Refuse to consider that this one shaky assumption is a sign that all the major assumptions should be seriously questioned. Instead, maintain one's strong emotional ties to the familiar package of beliefs. Next, try to arrive at a rewritten assumption for the one under attack. Perhaps an added footnote will account for this disturbing new evidence. Or, at worst, the problematic assumption will have to be rewritten, but in a form (no matter how awkward) that will let one hang on to all the rest of the old paradigm.

For example, what do we do when statistics show the rising incidence of cancer in our society? Do we question the entire package of assumptions—the stress created by "big is better" thinking, the sense of animosity created by a competitive economic system, the horrendous things we do to nature to extract the resources we demand? Here is a blatant anomaly that announces that something is not right with our style of living on planet Earth. But rather than look for a new set of assumptions, a strong tendency exists to hang on to the old world view and merely make some patchwork. So what happens? Medical science selects a few scapegoats; it finds several dozen substances that are carcinogenic. Then it announces that you can still be safe and healthy within the old paradigm *if* you just pay attention to the new footnote which warns, "Don't let yourself come in contact with any of these known cancer-causing substances."

By way of analogy, it's like a man with a leaking roof on his old house. He springs a leak in March and patches it up. But another one occurs in April and two in May. He keeps up this patchwork process, never considering that the time has come for a new roof. He can conceivably keep this up, but the day will come when his entire roof will be an awkward-looking array that is totally patchwork. The sum of his time and dollar expense in all that patchwork will be greater than if he had gotten a new roof.

Sometimes the patchwork looks ludicrous. Like the emperor with no clothes, the situation almost begs for someone to demand courageously, "How could that be?" But the stakes are high. If people are determined to hang on to the old mind-set, then the old assumptions with their new footnotes will do just fine, no matter how awkward it looks. In fact such people would even proudly point to such alterations as proof of their open-mindedness and willingness to change with the times.

Let's look at an example of this technique for handling changing times. The old theory that the Sun and planets travel around the Earth was a major assumption in the medieval paradigm. However, there were anomalies that should have alerted people to the fact that their view of reality was inadequate. For example, anyone who watched the planet Mars night after night would observe a strange phenomenon. It would seem to move gradually across the background of the fixed stars. Over the course of weeks and months, it would seem to be traveling through the various constellations of the sky. This progression was very much expected because people were sure that Mars was circling the Earth.

But occasionally Mars would do a curious thing—it would reverse its course and for several weeks seem to move backward. (A modern-day astrologer would call this a planet "going retrograde.") The observation, which could readily be made by anyone, seemed to cast doubt upon the assumption that the planets, the Sun, and the Moon were all revolving around the Earth. For many centuries after this retrograde motion was noticed, people were not willing to part with the assumptions of their paradigm. It was difficult to ignore the evidence of an anomaly; therefore, the next best technique was employed. They patched up the old assumption, and the theory was changed. According to the revised notion, the Earth was still the center of the Solar System, but some of the planets did not traverse a circular, or even elliptical, orbit around the Earth; rather, planets like Mars traveled with a periodic loop-de-loop in their paths! In the next illustration we see first the pathway Mars would appear to take as one watched it over the weeks move against the background of the fixed stars. The second illustration shows the "patched-up" assumption—the belief adopted by those who weren't willing to create a new paradigm.

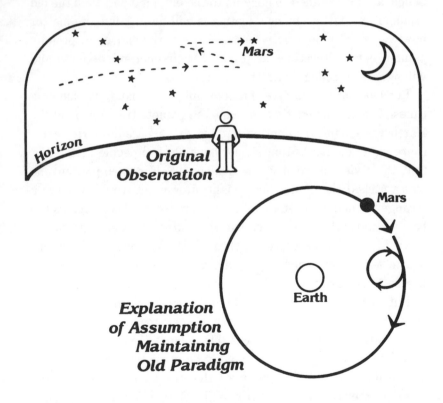

The idea of such an orbital pathway seems ludicrous to us with our modern knowledge of astronomy. But what else could the people of that day do? Their worldview and mind-set were too precious for them to seriously consider new assumptions. It was not until the Renaissance that a sensible idea of the Solar System was generally accepted and the retrograde motion of the planets was easily explained. The relative difference in speed between the Earth's movement around the Sun and that of another planet like Mars would create the occasional *appearance* of backward movement.

We can laugh at the people six hundred years ago in their naivete and stubbornness. But isn't it possible that six hundred years from now our descendants will view some of *our* patched-up assumptions as equally amusing? To what degree do *we* now try to modify old assumptions to avoid having to develop an entirely different worldview? Or, in what ways do we take something that is of the new world and distort it so that it looks like part of the old world? When the world is changing in the way ours is now, such methods can only temporarily slow the movement. People who would hang on to the old assumptions may still be in the majority but the evolution of consciousness on this planet doesn't depend on majority vote. If it did, then things would never really move forward. Human fears and desires would keep us stuck. **Paradigm shifts on the scale of the Renaissance happen *in spite of* the majority.**

Those who insist on trying various methods to *maintain* the old set of assumptions will find the coming decades to be especially troublesome. They are likely to feel the inner millennium shift most accutely. The temporizing, patching up, denying techniques won't work for long. They, like all of us, will have to face the new world being born around them, and more importantly being born within themselves.

Joining the Emergent Paradigm

In response to inner and outer millennium shifts, we can choose to work cooperatively with a new set of values and assumptions. Cayce predicted that some individuals would be pioneers of a new planetary consciousness. Who are those people and how can we recognize them in today's world?

They are the ones who sense that the old ways are dying and can sense a fresh orientation for humanity and planet Earth. They are people who are generally patient and not driven by fears. They trust that there is a plan to what is going on in the world, that there is a spirit of the times that is in keeping with God's plan. They know themselves to be cocreators with God in the transformation to a new worldview, but they humbly recognize that their work is to respond to the divine initiative which will be revealed to them.

What are the characteristics of such a person? In fact, *such an individual is within each of us.* All of us have the potential to be among those who make this kind of response to the inner millennium shift. All of us have the capability of being *receptive* in these times, which is a first characteristic of this sort of person. This isn't passivity, because the builders of twenty-first century culture need to be active and involved. Rather it's a matter of listening before acting. By way of an analogy, it's like being a swimmer in open waters and taking the time to become aware of the position and direction of a current. Once that perception is made, one can then actively swim in the current and be carried along by it. It's a matter of being able to sense the true spirit of these times. Such listening must reach beneath the surface of current events in the outer world.

The true spirit of these times isn't the fear of being down-sized, social unrest, or even earth changes. There will be many *symptoms* of what is going on, but we need to look deeper to see the real spirit of what is being born. In fact, **the nightly television news is more likely to document the dying of the old world than the birth of the new.** A real listener—a real cocreator of the world Cayce predicted for the twenty-first century—senses the elements emerging for a new paradigm. He or she then acts in response to what has been noticed. That person is able to give expression and form to the new assumptions about life.

This sort of person—who is within us all as a potential—is also able to put aside fears. He or she is able courageously to accept that moment of void we encounter when we have let go of the old and yet the new isn't yet fully within our grasp. We might wonder what it is that most scares people about times of change and paradigm shifts. Do we fear that the future might be worse than the past has been? Or rather, are we more afraid of the void—of that moment of uncertainty and vulnerability—when the old assumptions have faded but we are not yet clear about the new? We need the confidence of a trapeze artist who has let go of one swing and momentarily hangs helplessly out in space before grabbing on to the next: he knows his own momentum will carry him forward to meet the swing he trusts will be there.

In many arenas of life, people confront the difficulties posed by that void—for example, in their vocations and in their choices about close personal relationships. Many individuals stick with an old job even though they cannot imagine having any other job that would be more distasteful to them. But they are afraid to quit—oftentimes not so much worried that they would remain unemployed as because they cannot stand the thought of being in that uncertain, vulnerable void for any amount of time. It takes courage to move on to a new vocation, a new set of friends, or a whole new set of assumptions for living. The capacity to overcome the fear is within each of us.

Another characteristic of the person who embraces the new paradigm is an alchemical type of skill. The alchemists of ancient times attempted to turn lead into gold. Or, more accurately, they tried to transform the base or earthly aspects of human consciousness into enlightenment. A version of this skill belongs to the pioneers of the millennium. Some things viewed as weaknesses by the old set of assumptions can be seen as strengths by the new paradigm.

Cayce was especially skillful at showing individuals how this transformative principle could work at a personal level. He often described how a fault could be lifted into a strength. For example, one man who came to Cayce on many occasions was known to be extremely talkative, often to the annoyance of those around him.

However, Cayce pointed out how this fault could be alchemically transmuted into a great strength as he became an eloquent and eager spokesperson for spiritual truth.

Certainly not everything held in low esteem by the old paradigm will suddenly be much admired in the new one. It's the skill of the cocreators of a new world to recognize and work with those qualities that are good candidates for the alchemical change. Let us consider two examples.

One candidate is sensitivity. In the old world it's often considered a weakness to be sensitive. In the competitive worlds of our vocations, the sensitive person is likely to get ulcers. Sensitivity generally runs counter to the assumption that there are limited resources and one had better be tough to struggle hard for his own share. But in a new paradigm, sensitivity can be transformed from weakness to strength. For example, a requirement for leadership in the twenty-first century may be sensitivity to others.

Another candidate is interdependence. This is a good illustration of the process at work on a global scale. In the old paradigm, it's weakness for one nation to be dependent on another nation. For example, we say that the United States has a weakness in requiring the oil of the Persian Gulf countries. We say that Belgium is a weak nation because it's dependent upon France, Germany and the United States for military protection. And by old world assumptions these instances and many more are true. However, with a new paradigm the assumptions have changed. Now we can see that we are one people on planet Earth. What benefits the people of one nation can potentially benefit those throughout the world. Our interdependence becomes a strength, alchemically transformed into a stimulus for cooperation. A characteristic once held in low esteem can become something that is newly admired and appreciated. Cayce described this principle to one man, intent on being a leader in the creation of a new world: ". . . as has been given of old, 'That stone that was rejected of the builders has become the cornerstone . . . '" (#900–318). Such is the work of the builders of a new world—to recognize and nurture the qualities of life that can go through such a dramatic switch.

Finally, pioneers of the twenty-first century culture that Cayce envisioned will treat with respect the elements of the old paradigm. They won't be angry or full of hatred, simply allowing the old worldview to run its course and die. Instead it's with love that they take the elements of the old ways and find new places for them. It's a crucial point to understand. Remember that when we moved to a new gestalt (for example, seeing the two faces instead of the goblet), the literal elements of the scene did not change. Instead it was our way of ordering them that was altered. We created new priorities, putting the background into the foreground. Or when we stretched a square into the higher dimensional life of being a cube, we did not destroy the square. We merely changed the relative importance and priority of its position.

The same must hold true if we are to move properly from a world run by the old paradigm to a world run by the new. Many of the elements of living will remain. The challenge is to arrange, order and relate them to each other based on a new set of rules. Cayce's prophecies about the coming centuries make clear that we will still have families, businesses, governments, schools and agriculture. The shift in paradigms doesn't mean eliminating business just because it may have been poorly operated under the old set of assumptions. Nor does it mean throwing out the idea of governments just because wars and hatreds were created when governments operated under the old rules of the game.

Inner millennium shift is essentially a changing gestalt, a new way of arranging priorities and relationships. This is far more challenging than just watching the old world die. The current transformation isn't so much one in which the individual elements of the scene change; it's rather the emergence of a new gestalt that sees those elements in entirely new relationships. And with this new set of priorities, a different and more productive way of living can also be born. That's what the millennium—inner *and* outer—is really all about.

Chapter 8

LIVING CREATIVELY WITH INNER EARTH CHANGES

Where is the real cutting edge for these times of change? Technological advancements, changing roles for women, shifts in the balance of political power? These and countless other factors are playing crucial roles. But Cayce's millennium prophecies point to something else: the changes to take place *within each individual.* The inner levels are where people experience and deal with cultural and physical transformations. That's the cutting edge, and it's far more significant than anything else, including earthquakes. According to these prophecies, the outer will largely be shaped by the inner. In the way people collectively deal with the *inner* millennium shift, the *outer* forms will be created for us to experience.

In the previous chapter we examined Cayce's philosophy that God is dynamic and fosters change. We also identified an opportunity that each of us can accept when the world around us is being transformed: the chance to become a cocreator, to be sensitive to an emerging, new paradigm and embrace it. In this chapter we will venture farther in that direction and try to answer the question, *"Exactly how can we begin to prepare ourselves right now to become people who will cocreate a new world?"* In other words, what's the next step for those willing to make a paradigm shift?

There are, in fact, disciplines to prepare ourselves for the work of building a new world, exercises that Cayce mentioned time and again to people interested in preparing themselves for the future. A trio of disciplines makes up the Cayce formula for those who want to help build the kind of world in the next millennium that he envisioned.

First, nothing is more important than clarifying our ideals and purposes. We must see unquestionably what we hold as core values. Our purposes and motives must be carefully chosen. Otherwise, powerful forces from the media and mass culture easily hypnotize us into settling for less than our best. It's truly an act of will to choose and commit to an ideal with positive vision about the world's possibilities.

Second is purifying and attuning our physical bodies. The birth of a new, planetary culture will happen at this physical dimension. And how can we be participants—even helpers—in its birth unless we have healthy bodies with which to be involved? The stresses of changing times hit the body hard. Through nutrition and exercise we must diligently work to do the best we can with our own physical bodies.

A third crucial discipline is meditation, the daily practice of inner and outer peace. As we'll see, it's deeply linked to our values and ideals. What's more, meditation is a powerful tool for creating health for our physical bodies.

Let's look at each of these three in sequence—setting values and ideals, attuning the physical body, and meditating.

Discipline #1: Setting Ideals and Core Values

The power of intentions and values is indispensable to our creative response to inner earth changes. The exercise of self-evaluation and the setting of ideals is something Cayce encouraged people to do on a regular basis. Many people find that a yearly discipline of reviewing core values works best—perhaps around New Year's

Day or near one's own birthday. Setting ideals is a matter of carefully formulating the motives and intentions that you want to have guiding and directing your life. We can designate ideals that are spiritual, mental, or physical.

What did Cayce mean by the phrase "spiritual ideal"? It's not so much a goal or accomplishment that we hope to achieve, but instead refers to the *purpose* behind our actions or the *spirit* in which we approach the challenges and opportunities of life.

This is the question to ask yourself in setting a spiritual ideal: "What spirit of living do I want directing every part of my life?" In other words, ask yourself what sense of meaning and purpose you want to strive for in the way you live. What's the *core value or quality* you wish to have guiding your life? Of course, not every action, thought, or feeling will reflect that ideal, because in our humanness we often fall short. But each of us can aspire to a profound sense of meaning—a higher way of seeing life and others and self. As you determine your spiritual ideal, be sure it comes from deep within yourself and not from the expectations of others. In other words, a spiritual ideal for your life must not have a quality of "ought" or "should." Throughout our lives, our parents, teachers, and other authority figures tell us what our purposes and aspirations in life ought to be. A true spiritual ideal comes more authentically from your own self.

How can this deeper, more genuine level be tapped? One way is to draw upon the peak spiritual moments you have already had in your life. Each of us has caught glimpses—however briefly—of a higher spiritual reality. Each of us has tasted a deeper, more profound sense of purposefulness to life than the perspective offered by conscious physical life.

What were the peak spiritual moments of your past? They may have been one or two special dreams in which you seemed to be touched by a higher reality. They may have been deep prayer and meditation experiences. Your peak spiritual moments may even have been in waking life—a loving moment with someone, a day of heightened creativity, or a special time out in nature. Think back over your life and recall several such special times. They are moments to be honored deeply and remembered, even though the busyness of daily living causes you to forget or ignore the impact they once had upon you.

To choose a spiritual ideal then, take several minutes to sit quietly and remember these peak spiritual moments. Try to relive them and let these memories shape your thinking and feeling so that for a moment you become the person you were in those special experiences. Once you are in touch with that different place within yourself, allow into your mind a word or phrase that describes that state of consciousness. For one person, the spiritual ideal might be "loving freedom"; for another person, it might be "oneness with the Light"; and for still a third, simply "service." No matter what words you use, they should describe a place of consciousness within yourself that you have actually touched and tasted. A spiritual ideal must be something living for you—not merely a philosophical abstraction.

In setting a spiritual ideal this way, you may sense that even higher ideals are possible. In fact, one's spiritual ideal is, in effect, a statement that affirms, "This is the highest meaning and purpose of life that I know as reality, because I have personally been touched by it."

A spiritual ideal—as it has just been described—relates to our highest *aspirations*. Clearly, in the Cayce philosophy of how to deal with inner earth changes, having high aspirations is crucial. But just as important is another ingredient: *trust*. Think about how you might aspire to something but not trust that it is alive within you, not trust that it is possible to experience for yourself. Without investing yourself through trust, you haven't genuinely set a spiritual ideal.

This may not be a point of view that's easy to swallow, simply because most of us find trusting to be very difficult. To trust requires a more challenging use of free will than does aspiration alone. Trust means a willingness to surrender and let go of fears and doubts. It means to place ultimate belief in forces beyond your personal, conscious self. You haven't yet set a spiritual ideal until you let go and put your trust in it.

Here is a somewhat superficial example that will remind you of *what it feels like* to trust. When you turn on a light, you trust that the electricity will be there, ready to light up the room. When you turn the handle on the faucet, you trust that the water will start flowing. In other words, you probably spend little of your day worrying about the availability of power and water. Now, of course, a critic could say that you're taking it for granted—that many people in the world don't have immediate access to these resources. But the point here is not the fact that we are very fortunate. Instead, these examples teach us something about trust: when you trust, it brings the freedom to act without the burden of worry or doubt.

The authentic ideal you hold is the one you don't have to spend time thinking about or questioning. It has become so much a part of your life that it's a "given." When you meet a difficulty or a challenge, *you know you can count on the inspiration and power of that ideal* just as surely as you count on electricity and water when you need them. Some days your genuine ideal has the quality of being almost invisible to you because it's so deeply a part of how you look at the world. It's so essential that you don't stop to question it or worry about it.

Once we have carefully set a personal spiritual ideal—choosing a word or phrase that has deep, evocative power for us—then it is helpful to make that spiritual ideal a little "closer to home" by selecting companion mental ideals and physical ideals. They are the more pragmatic steps for how we'll put that spiritual ideal into application. Actually writing them down is a good idea because it forces us to be specific.

Mental ideals are designated attitudes and feelings, which we hope to keep in mind as often as possible, that we know will be stepping-stones toward a fuller expression of our spiritual ideal. In the midst of a difficult relationship, one might choose tolerance as a mental ideal because an attitude that accepts the other person's point of view without judgment may be the first step toward the spiritual ideal that has been set.

In a similar way, our actions and behaviors can be stepping-stones. These optimal ways of behaving in the world are what Cayce called physical ideals. In the midst of that same difficult relationship, one might commit to a daily morning prayer for the other person because this would be a stepping-stone toward tolerance and toward the spiritual ideal chosen. Of course, there's room for change, and we're likely to amend our list of mental ideals and physical ideals on a regular basis, as a response to the variety of difficult people who come into our lives or to the challenging new problems that arise.

For example, here's what one forty-five-year-old man identified as his ideals in the midst of a chaotic world. Revisiting five of his own peak spiritual experiences—two special dreams, a potent meditation experience, and two extraordinary moments in nature—he arrived at the phrase "centered peace" for a spiritual ideal. When it came to setting mental and physical ideas, he focused on two challenging parts of his life. First was a difficult relationship at work, a man whose behavior was constantly a source of annoyance. Although "peace centeredness" seemed like a stretch for him in that relationship, he picked "tolerance" as a mental ideal—that is, a stepping-stone toward his spiritual ideal. As a physical ideal he made a commitment to prayer for that man each day.

For a second area of challenge he selected his relationship with his own body, which often seemed to be restless and unhealthy, anything but "peacefully centered." As a step toward that spiritual ideal, he identified "appreciation" as a mental ideal. Simply the attitude of being grateful for his body seemed like it would be a constructive step. For a physical ideal he decided that a couple of life-style changes would be a positive move: trying to get to bed by 10:30 at least six nights a week, and making sure that he drank at least six glasses of water a day.

As he made progress with these mental and physical ideals, this man could expect to stretch himself a little more with mental and physical ideals that would take him closer to his spiritual ideal, both in those two parts of his life *and* in additional challenging situations.

Even when we've set high ideals, often we never get around to doing much about them. Too easily we get distracted or pulled off onto detours. In fact, *inner earth changes often create enormous distractions that try to siphon off our spiritual vitality.* It would be well for most of us to examine our lives closely and see how we may use distractions to avoid putting energy into drawing nearer to our ideals. The effect of most distractions is to put our lives on "hold." They are ways of tuning out most of the world and retreating to an awareness that does not challenge us at the growth points of our souls. And certainly our society offers many opportunities for this. Some of the ways are overt, such as drugs—whether we mean tranquilizers, alcohol, cocaine, marijuana or whatever. It isn't hard to see that these sorts of things can put barriers between ourselves and God by disengaging us from the mature ways that we can experience soul growth. But modern society offers lots of other consciousness-dulling distractions, too.

In the book *Brave New World*, Aldous Huxley presents a rather dim view of what the future might hold. Perhaps no book other than George Orwell's *1984* has had such a sobering effect on those of us who are taking a serious look at where the future may be leading us. In Huxley's literary imagination people routinely use a drug called "soma" which puts them into a stupor or transports them to a soothing fantasy.

What is the "soma" of our times? We might observe some scary parallels between the effects of soma in *Brave New World* and television in our world. Both allow people to unplug their minds from what is actually before them. Both can easily become avoidance mechanisms. We might consider the degree to which television watching has become for each of us a daily habit that has begun to interfere with our relationship with God. It isn't so much the content of what we watch—although that can be significant for various reasons, too—but that the process of *disengaging our minds from the reality of our personal lives* is a distraction which for some people stands directly in the way of spiritual growth.

Another kind of distraction for some people is sports. Even participatory sports, with their exercise and health benefits, become a spiritual problem if taken to an extreme. But the larger problem is spectator sports, in which people are "drugged" into believing that the "games" being enacted before them are somehow more important than anything else in their lives.

Somehow men are particularly vulnerable to this kind of psychology. Ask someone who has succumbed to this type of distraction and he will say that his wife, children, home and job are much more important to him than his favorite football team. But watch his emotions and his behavior. Sometimes you might not be sure what his priorities really are.

No matter what you have placed between yourself and God, it's to your advantage to discover it. Without such self-discovery, it's very hard to stay focused on your real priorities and ideals. In times of inner change, these distractions will be points at which pressure is put on your life to grow and change.

Discipline #2: Ideals-Centered Meditation

Meditation is a second practical key to creative living in the midst of inner earth changes. In Cayce's philosophy, meditation doesn't mean blanking out the mind or engaging in pleasant fantasy. Meditation is a word reserved for a very purposeful, specific spiritual discipline. That discipline involves a focused effort to experience deeply the reality and power of one's own spiritual ideal.

Many books have been written about ideals-centered meditation, based on Cayce's philosophy and the meditation principles of like-minded teachers. The practice is simple and easy to learn. Meditation differs from prayer in that meditation involves *quieting* the conscious mind and being alert for inspiration and renewal. In contrast, prayer is a purposeful *activity* of the conscious mind.

In Cayce's approach to meditation, one selects a short statement of the spiritual ideal—what he calls an "affirmation"—and uses those few words to move into a closer and deeper experience of the reality and vitality of this core value. The words you choose should have a powerful, evocative quality—they need to be able to awaken strong *feelings* for the spiritual ideal. Consider one example of an affirmation: if you had chosen "Love" as your spiritual ideal, an appropriate affirmation for meditation might be something such as "Let me always be a channel of blessings and love to others." The affirmation becomes a *focal point of attention* during the silence of meditation. What Cayce refers to as an affirmation is very similar to what is called a "mantra" (or "mind tool") in certain Eastern meditation systems.

What words should you choose for your affirmation? Other than writing your own, you might take a favorite line from the Bible (e.g., "Be still and know that I am God") or from other sacred scripture. Some meditators keep their affirmations quite brief and, in fact, use only the short phrase they have selected for their spiritual ideal.

Most people find that between ten and twenty minutes of quiet, uninterrupted time is required for each meditation session. What's more, regularity—preferably on a daily basis at about the same time—works best. Sitting comfortably, you can do whatever helps to get into a centered, purposeful frame of mind: listening to sooth-ing or inspiring music for a few minutes, reading from sacred literature, or taking a few moments for prayer, either aloud or silent.

You may find it helpful at the beginning of your meditation session to create in your mind some visual imagery that relates to your affirmation and helps you get in touch with it. For example, some meditators find it helpful to imagine themselves sitting in a special spiritual place. The image of that setting then allows them to identify more quickly with the life purpose that the affirmation represents.

As you center your mind and move into the quiet of meditation, focus your attention on the words of the affirmation and any images you're using. Do this until you begin to experience the feeling and spirit behind the words. You are using your conscious will to concentrate and keep your attention one-pointed. However, the effort you make to direct attention is not an intellectual effort to dissect the affirmation or analyze the images. Instead, let your attention rest upon the *feeling and spirit* the affirmation begins to call forth from your unconscious mind. This stage may require much practice because of the strong tendency for your attention to drift off to distracting thoughts and emotions.

Once you have reached a point where you recognize that the affirmation has begun to do its work—that new feelings are being awakened—then drop the words and any images you have created. This is the silence of meditation. Here you rest in silent attention in the quiet spirit of the ideal your affirmation represents. At this point, words are unnecessary. They have done their job by getting you back in touch with another way of feeling and seeing yourself and life.

When your attention drifts, repeat the steps of focusing attention on the words, then let go of them once you have their spirit. In other words, you can expect that your capacity to stay in the silence will be limited. At first, you will probably find that after just ten or fifteen seconds of silently holding the feeling of your affirmation a distracting thought or emotion will grab your attention and pull you away. When you recognize you have been caught up in a distraction, go back to focusing on the affirmation until you reexperience its meaning and spirit. You may have to repeat this sequence many times in a single meditation session. Even experienced meditators have to go back frequently and reawaken to their sense of highest purpose by recalling the affirmation and then reattaining the silence.

As a final step, surrender all efforts to make something happen. All the previous steps have included effort on your part to direct the meditation session. Even if you have no expectations or desires for some special experience in meditation, conscious effort and the exercise of will has been necessary. However, the last phase of your meditation should include a short period during which you fully surrender, discontinuing all conscious effort. When you have spent sufficient time holding in silent attention the feeling and meaning of your affirmation, and you feel permeated by its spirit, *release even the affirmation.*

A good way to experience the surrender is to refocus your attention on your *breathing.* In other words, once you have let the meaning of your affirmation permeate both your conscious and unconscious, then spend several minutes in attentive breathing. This exercise at the close is not to force a change in consciousness by an extraordinary breathing technique. Instead, by letting your attention focus on something as simple as your breath, the power of what you have subconsciously achieved in the previous steps is able to touch you even more deeply.

The key to this final step is the word "surrender." There must be a sense of giving up (but not of "giving in")—letting go of all mental efforts to force something to happen.

Discipline #3: Right Diet and Nutrition

What we feed our bodies has a tremendous effect on our state of consciousness. Diet and nutrition is bound to be a key variable in our capacity to meet inner earth changes in a creative and hopeful way. If we chemically undermine the health of our bodies, we're sure to find the going very tough in these times of radical change. But if we give the cells of our bodies a balanced and vital source of energy, it will allow the best within us to emerge.

Cayce's readings spoke very often about diet and nutrition. In fact, two-thirds of his psychic material concerned health and healing, and the vast majority of his health readings included dietary suggestions for the recipient. At the time he offered his philosophy of nutrition, consciousness, and healing, it was considered revolutionary. But in the decades that have now passed, the best of nutritional science has started to sound more and more like Cayce's suggestions.

Two fundamental elements make up Cayce's diet recommendations: balance and food sources. Balance relates to the relative percentage of one's diet that comes from food that metabolizes to produce an acidic residue in the body. Such acid-reacting foods should make up about twenty percent of one's diet—the remaining eighty percent being foods that metabolize to create an alkaline residue. These two lists provide the general guidelines:

Acid-reacting foods:

Meats, animal fats and vegetable oils. Large prunes, plums, cranberries, and rhubarb. All cereal grains and their products such as bread, breakfast foods, rolled oats, polished rice, etc. (Brown rice is somewhat less acid forming.) All high-starch and protein foods. White sugar, syrups, nuts, peanuts, and coconut. Legumes (dried beans, dried peas, and lentils).

Alkaline-reacting foods:

All fruits, fresh and dried, except large prunes, plums, and cranberries. All vegetables, fresh and dehydrated, except legumes. All forms of milk, including buttermilk, clabber, sour milk, cottage cheese, and cheese.

Another aspect of nutritional balance concerns food combinations. It's not enough to work simply with the lists of acid and alkaline-reacting foods. One also has to be careful about combining certain foods in the same meal. Cayce's most frequent recommendations about combinations to *avoid* were

1. milk or cream in coffee
2. citrus fruits (including orange juice) and whole grains

3. milk and orange juice
4. starches and proteins

Food sources is the second fundamental element of Cayce's diet principles which can help us stay focused and healthy in stressful, changing times. Cayce often referred to the body as "the temple." If you were literally building a sacred temple, you would be very careful about the quality of the stones and other materials that went into that special structure. Just as surely, each of us ought to be vigilant concerning the quality of what goes into our mouths.

One important aspect to consider is purity. In an age of agribusiness and widespread use of potent pesticides, we may have to work hard to achieve the ideal purity we'd like to have for our diet. And even if one hundred percent pure, organically grown food seems to be an unreasonable stretch, one can still strive for a certain target percentage that has a high purity standard. And don't forget pure water—six to eight glasses per day.

By food sources Cayce also meant the locale from which it comes. He encouraged us to try to find local sources of food, suggesting that food grown near our own town or city might vibrationally be easier to assimilate. Another advantage of locally grown (or better yet, homegrown) fruits and vegetables is that of vitamin retention. Cayce pointed out how certain foods lose a considerable portion of their nutritional value in the days following harvesting; and often, food grown locally is available to us much closer to the date on which it was harvested. For this reason—plus the wonderful effects that come from getting one's own hands in the soil—having a small garden at home is highly desirable.

Along with the other two disciplines of ideals and meditation, careful attention to nutrition can make an extraordinary difference in one's life. These three methods, advocated time and again by Cayce, can allow us to have the clarity, vitality, and strength to meet the stresses and uncertainty of these times. All three of these disciplines take practice and patience with oneself. For some individuals they probably need to be phased in gradually. But with consistence of practice, these three methods will produce powerful results and allow us to fully participate in building the most creative possibilities for the new millennium.

Cayce's Errors and the Flexibility of the Future

How realistic is it to expect that we as individuals can significantly shape the future? Disciplines such as setting ideals, attuning our bodies, and meditation can be expected to help us personally. But will they actually help create the *course of history* in the decades just ahead? Some say no. They assume that the future is already fixed and predetermined. Prophets such as Cayce can see that future, they claim, and there's not much we can do but prepare for it.

That's *not* the position that Cayce himself took in his readings about the future. Conditions for the twenty-first century and beyond aren't predetermined. Yes, there may be strong trends and likelihoods. Even the overall shape of things may be largely set, just as a human embryo already has the patterns that will create its appearance at birth. But there is still room to influence that development.

Ironically, it's instances in which Cayce's predictions seem to have been wrong that should give us a measure of hope that we can still make a difference. He was not one hundred percent accurate in his prophecies. Those examples suggest that perhaps the future is continually being shaped and that our own modest efforts have a role to play as the new millennium begins to emerge.

When we look at the Cayce prophecies with a critical eye, it's clear that some of the predictions have failed to come true, *at least within the timetable Cayce envisioned.* Those failures could potentially undermine our trust in his reliability. However, other influences may also contribute to the errors, too. Those additional factors conceivably relate to our own powers to help shape the future—powers that come through our attitudes and actions. One essential principle stands out in Cayce's statements about how we can still influence what's to come: our responses to the *inner* millennium shift significantly affect the way in which the *outer* changes play out.

Cayce's descendants and the serious students of his work haven't tried to hide his errors. There is no argument about the fact that the Cayce readings were fallible. Hugh Lynn Cayce and Edgar Evans Cayce have written a book documenting some of the cases in which their father was wrong. Entitled *The Outer Limits of Edgar Cayce's Power*, it has sold fewer copies than almost any other nationally-distributed book on his psychic work, perhaps because people generally do not want to hear about a psychic's errors.

Yet we cannot avoid this issue in a study of the earth changes prophecies. We must each consider what it is about this man's work that gives us reason to consider seriously his warnings. In fact, there are probably only two reasons for us to treat the earth changes readings with curiosity and respect. First is the remarkable convergence of Cayce's prophecies with those from other cultures and time periods—predictions of which Cayce had no conscious knowledge. Many of them were outlined in Chapter 6. Corroborative evidence is one of the reliable tools used by scientists and researchers in many academic disciplines. In this case, the parallels strongly suggest that we take Cayce's millennium prophecies seriously.

Second is the almost undeniable evidence that Cayce was a gifted psychic. His accuracy in diagnosing physical ailments was astounding. There is a remarkable frequency of dramatic health improvements in people who followed the individualized recommendations they had received in their readings. The sheer volume of accurate physical readings is a persuasive reason to take seriously the statements he made in readings outside the scope of health care.

Of course positive research findings about his medical clairvoyant powers do not prove anything about his views of history, his dream interpretations or prophecies of earth changes. To a large measure, each of the areas in which Cayce gave readings needs to stand on its own for testing. By analogy, just because your general practitioner gave you good advice for healing a sprained ankle, would you automatically trust him or her for brain surgery? Of course not, because physicians typically have areas of specialty. There might be some excellent brain surgeons who also have a general practice, but we cannot assume that is always the case.

So let's briefly consider instances in which specific Cayce predictions failed to materialize. Most of the prophecies do *not* have specific dates associated with them. For this reason, it is usually difficult to judge whether or not they are correct. If a psychic says, "Someday Los Angeles will be destroyed by an earthquake," it can never be proved wrong. If that psychic says that between 1958 and 1998 we can expect to see Los Angeles destroyed, then at least we will be able to evaluate the information by 1998. There were a few cases, however, in which Cayce gave specific dates for major changes to happen. As we've already seen, events for 1936 is a good case in point because several things Cayce predicted failed to occur. In another instance, regarding the rising of the hypothetical lost continent of Atlantis, Cayce referred in 1940 to specific dates in the future: "And Poseidia will be among the first portions of Atlantis to rise again. Expect it in sixty-eight and sixty-nine ('68 and '69); not so far away!" (#958–3). There is currently no clear evidence to suggest that this prophecy was fulfilled. Some investigators feel that they found underwater in the late 1960s evidence of the ruins of a civilization near Bimini. This claim is still arguable; and the fact remains that Cayce predicted the *rising of land* in 1968 and 1969—something which seems fairly certain not to have happened.

All of these instances in which Cayce prophecies appear to be wrong may be interpreted and analyzed from a variety of perspectives. In fact there are alternatives, at least *three* ways in which we can approach the problem created by the mistaken readings just cited. More than just an intellectual exercise, a careful look at these alternatives addresses the key theme for this chapter: is the immediate future something that can still be influenced or changed, and if so, how?

First, let's consider the nature of time and the possibility that Cayce's errors were primarily a misperception of timing. Many theorists who speculate about higher-dimensional reality feel that time, as we understand it, is probably a quality of only this three-dimensional, physical world. Perhaps Cayce was in a place of higher-dimensional consciousness, where likely events in physical space appeared accurately to his perception, and yet their location in time was clouded or ambiguous. This would suggest that even the events that were predicted and did not happen may yet come to pass.

However, other approaches have also been proposed in order to explain the apparent errors. A second possibility is that many of these prophecies are symbolic in nature. In other words, could it be that in 1926 California and Japan did experience jolting changes—if not geological, then perhaps economic, social or political? Could it be that 1936 was a year in which the poles *did* shift— not the literal rotation of the earth, but the spiritual, economic or political equilibrium of the world? Did "Atlantean consciousness" rise to the surface in 1968 and 1969? These were particularly turbulent years of social unrest in Western society, and a case might be made that a certain frame of mind (symbolized by the mythic image of Atlantis) determined not to let the world go down a pathway of self-destruction.

The symbolism explanation is attractive because it challenges us to look at the Cayce prophecies in a broader scope—to identify the themes and patterns in his statements, finding the teaching quality of his message much as we would from a parable of Jesus or one of Aesop's Fables. It requires us to recognize a big picture in what Cayce's inner source was trying to convey, even if the man Edgar Cayce fell short of being able to articulate it accurately.

Perhaps land rising in the Bahamas in 1968 or 1969 was the best that Cayce could do to convey the visionary images that came from his superconscious mind. He wasn't a perfect channel of his inspiration—by his own admission—and when words and dates had to be found, perhaps he sometimes came up short. It's easy to see why a visionary like Nostradamus may have preferred to make his predictions in poetic terms that maintained a good measure of the ambiguity that presumably accompanies the mystic's view of the mundane world.

How then are we to judge the wisdom of a seer? Something invaluable is sure to be missed if all we can do is judge by reductionism. What happens if our evaluation of Cayce's statements about 1926, 1936 or 1968–69 are reduced solely to questions such as "Did the earth's literal axis of rotation alter in 1936?" or "Did a dry land with twelve-thousand-year-old architectural ruins surface in 1968 from the water of the Bahamas?" The purely physical answers here are "no." But we should be more sophisticated seekers of meaning and wisdom. By considering the symbolic themes that Cayce used, we may find significant insight and truth even in the predictive statements that some critics have dismissed as obvious errors.

However, in spite of how attractive this symbolic interpretation may be, it has its dangers. It's tempting to misuse it and come out treating Cayce as a cult figure—someone who could never be wrong. Cayce himself knew better and never wanted such treatment. He realized that his readings were sometimes distorted or contaminated with false impressions. In the back of our own minds—even as we give serious consideration to a symbolic interpretation of some millennium prophecy readings—we need to remember that possibility for error.

We are left, then, with at least one other approach—perhaps the most insightful and promising one. This point of view suggests that "something happened" between many of Cayce's predictions and the date on which they were to have taken place. For example, most of the predictions about 1936 were made in the period from 1932–1934. Could it be that between 1934 and 1936 changes took place that altered the previewed course of events? This approach presupposes a notion of prophecy that is probably very sound: that the future is not fixed and predictions can only be statements of likelihood or probabilities. The course of events is like a train rushing down the tracks, with various forks in the tracks representing alternatives. At each fork the switch has been set in one position or another. Unless someone changes a switch, that train will follow a foreseeable path.

The Cayce readings themselves present this picture of prophecy. There is repeated reference to the way in which the actions and attitudes of humanity will shape the course of the future. The exact mechanism by which we could have such an effect is still somewhat of a mystery, but later in this chapter we'll examine one theory about how the thoughts and actions of even a relatively small percentage of humanity could alter the decision-making process of world leaders to enhance the prospects for peace. We'll also consider a way in which the thoughts of humanity may even influence the forces of nature. For the moment, perhaps a basic principle from the Cayce philosophy is sufficient: the universe is an interrelated whole, and part of this connected universe is the unseen realm of thought energy. In other words, what we experience as physical reality is primarily a result of what has been collectively built by humanity at the level of thought or consciousness.

But how, then, could the readings have occasionally been wrong? If Cayce's psychic gift allowed him to see clearly into this causative realm of thought energy, how could he have been mistaken about 1926, 1936 and 1968–69? One theory to explain the errors is that new thoughts are continually being created. If sufficient numbers of people change their consciousness after a prophecy has been given, then they might redirect the flow of events which materialize in the physical world. This is certainly the biblical notion of prophecy. The Old Testament spokesmen of God always had the same message: change your ways *or else* a destruction or calamity will befall you. In the story of the prophet Jonah, the people of Ninevah *did* alter their ways, and the catastrophe was averted.

It's to the credit of the Cayce readings that in at least one case they detected the changing course of events. We have seen the rather dramatic way in which Cayce's detailed prophecies concerning 1936 proved to be wrong. However, in January of 1936 at least one reading showed that Cayce had a new view of what was to take place that year. He specifically stated that the tremendous earthquake previously forecast for San Francisco would *not happen* that year. Unfortunately, he provided no explanation as to why the prophecy had changed.

Cayce had a dynamic, changeable vision of prophecy. Whereas in 1933 Cayce predicted an earthquake in San Francisco of unprecedented proportions, by January of 1936 he correctly saw that this was not going to happen. We are left to wonder if he simply had blurred psychic vision in 1933 which got clearer as the target date approached, or if some changes in the consciousness of people began to steer world events in a new direction. The latter of these two alternatives is much more challenging and exciting. It makes us *participants* in these times of transition.

The notion of participating in the building process of a new millennium is crucial. If we must sit back and wait for things to happen to us, then these times of change become all the more frightening. But with a sense of our own creative powers, the difficulties can be met with hope.

We have a responsibility for how history will unfold. This is true not only for questions on international warfare, population and the distribution of food resources, but even for the geological and geographical changes that may or may not come to pass. It's vital that we accept this sense of responsibility. And for this very reason, it's the third alternative that we should pursue most intently—this one that asserts that prophecies sometimes fail because human choices have set another form of the future in motion. It says that *the creative potential of human consciousness is more powerful than the psychic power of the prophet.* It shifts the focus away from anxieties about proving Cayce's psychic gift, and toward the responsibilities we all have in shaping the future. The third alternative is the one that deserves our attention because it puts the ultimate responsibility on us. It is actually the beginning of a much needed redefinition of "psychic." It says that the "professional psy-chic" isn't the only one who can "tune in" to likely future events; the psychic realm is the level on which all of us are operating *as we actively create the future together.*

We Can Make a Difference

Cayce's most important millennium prophecy unequivocally asserts that *we can make a difference* as humanity collectively creates its future. That's why this book has directed so much atten-tion to the *inner* millennium shift. As we find creative ways to meet these personal changes, we help to build a more balanced, harmonious way for the outer millennium shift to unfold. Cayce had a down-home way of making this point: "The little leaven can leaven the whole lump." It's a powerful principle: a few spiritually attuned souls can lift the consciousness of all humanity.

This philosophy has been called the principle of "critical mass." We're likely to have heard this term in a much more gruesome context: the explosion of an atomic bomb. To build a fission weapon, physicists know that it requires a threshold amount of certain radioactive substances, such as one form of uranium. If we have less than that threshold amount, no explosion can happen. But once we reach the threshold point—that is, the critical mass—something can suddenly start to happen.

The process is illustrated in the graph on the next page. The broken line represents our common thinking which says, "The effect I get out is in direct proportion to the amount I put in." In fact, many aspects of life follow this kind of relationship. However, in contrast, the solid line represents a process controlled by the princi-ple of critical mass. If we look carefully, we'll see that other essential aspects of life follow this alternative rule.

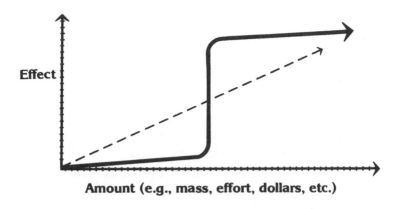

Amount (e.g., mass, effort, dollars, etc.)

Let's consider examples for each of the two. Some people find that the amount of food they eat has an effect on their weight, which roughly follows the broken line. Or, the number of dollars you pay per month in rent may be directly proportional to the quality of dwelling in which you live. Or, the amount of time you spend studying for a test will have a direct, proportional effect on your test score. (Of course, a more accurate depiction of many life experiences would be a curve approximating the broken line. The line would rise proportionately at first, but the concept of diminishing returns would set in and the line would begin to curve and then flatten out.)

But let's pause at the example of studying for a test. Suppose you are stuck in your learning by not understanding a particular key concept. If you study one or two hours, it may look pretty hopeless for the test tomorrow. Your score will be low, and furthermore, the difference will be very slight between having studied for one hour versus two hours. But imagine that it takes three hours to crack the difficult concept. Suddenly at the three-hour point that elusive concept becomes clear, and now you have the insight to be able to solve what had seemed to be impossible problems. Your score now is likely to be very high. Additional study beyond that may help a little bit more, but not very significantly. To put this into a chart we have:

Hours of Study	Effect (i.e., test score)
1	45
2	47
3	85
4	87

This is a classic example of critical mass or the threshold effect. Here's another commonplace example: running water into a bathtub that has no overflow protection drain, and then measuring the amount of water that has spilled out onto the bathroom floor. For the first five minutes in which the faucet runs there is no spilling effect upon the floor. But suddenly the critical point is reached—in this case the seventy-five-gallon capacity of the bathtub.

In Cayce's estimation, the future of planetary consciousness will be shaped by a critical mass type of curve. And significantly, he never suggests that the future of the world will be shaped by a majority vote. It will not take 51 percent of humanity in order to create a dramatic change in planetary awareness. The critical mass effect can be initiated by a relatively small number of people. That "little leaven" which can lift consciousness in all humanity may be just a handful of people compared to the earth's population.

The teachings of the Bible, as well as the philosophy of the Cayce readings, indicate that this has happened before. Recall the story of Abraham at the time just before the destruction of Sodom and Gomorrah. God warns Abraham that this destruction will take place because of the selfishness of people in those cities. What is Abraham's response? He attempts to bargain with God. He wonders, "If fifty righteous people can be found, would the cities be saved?" God's response is yes, that for the sake of the fifty, the city will not be destroyed. And then Abraham proceeds to find out just how far God will go in His offer of mercy—forty-five, forty, thirty, twenty, ten? Yes, God says, even if only ten righteous people can be found, the principle of critical mass will produce a saving effect on the entire populace of the cities. Ten was the threshold amount. Unfortunately it appears from the story that even those few could not be located.

In another illustration, the Cayce readings speak of the ancient Jewish sect called the Essenes as having served as a critical mass. Historians tell us little about this group of people who lived before and during the time of Jesus. Much more is known about the larger sects of Jewish thought in those times: the Sadducees and the Pharisees. In fact, were it not for the discovery of the Dead Sea Scrolls near the ruins of an Essene community at Qumran, almost nothing would be known of them.

However, in Cayce's psychic vision of the past, the Essenes played a key role in the coming of the Christ. It was this group who prepared themselves as a channel for the Messiah's entrance. Over many decades of practicing physical, mental and spiritual purification, they became a leaven that acted upon the consciousness of the planet. According to the Cayce readings, it was largely through the work of this relatively small group—both Mary and Joseph among them—that the Christ incarnated as Jesus. Apparently there were problems later. Jesus was not exactly the sort of savior they had planned for, and there may have been a break between Jesus and this community as He reached adulthood. However, in Cayce's visionary view of history, the fact remains that a threshold number of people—far, far smaller than any numerical majority—had an impact that was profoundly far-reaching.

And what, we might ask, are the numbers we are working with as we consider the possibility of "critical mass changes" in our own times? Perhaps the quantity will be similar to those of the past. How many Essenes did it require to create a channel for divine incarnation? Perhaps just several hundred. In biblical times we have seen that just ten righteous people were all that was required for a divine promise of mercy.

Two passages from Cayce's millennium prophecies—both given in June, 1940—mentioned specific numbers as threshold amounts for a quickening effect on the mass consciousness. When Cayce addressed the issue of why there was so much turmoil in the twentieth century world, he said that it was because people had forgotten God. It was not something that had to be, nor was it the karmic destiny of any nation or the planet as a whole. Then he went on to assert that the prayers *of even a single individual* can save a city.

In a second prophecy, given in that same reading (#3976–25), he promised a group of sixty-four people that they had the spiritual power to alter the course of America's destiny as World War II drew near for our nation: "For the prayer, and the living of same by those sixty and four who are here gathered, may even save America from being invaded—if that is what ye desire."

The first prophecy suggests that the threshold level for changing the future of a community or city is not even ten people, as the Old Testament story tells it. Instead, perhaps it is just *one* person who is attuned to God's will. The second passage is even more provocative. It was directed specifically to the sixty-four people gathered to hear a public reading by Cayce. This passage suggests a way of influencing the collective future of an entire nation. In this case, it was the threat that American territory would be invaded. We should note that World War II was already under way in Europe and the Far East, yet it was still a year and a half before the United States would be drawn in. Cayce's prophecy here in June of 1940 makes a bold assertion: if even sixty-four people pray and live in attunement with God's plan, then the likely future for the American people (an invasion) could be changed. Apparently the critical mass in consciousness was not achieved because the nation soon found its territory being invaded by aerial attack at Pearl Harbor less than two years later.

What's fascinating about this story is the report of one person who was present that day and recalls the discussion among the group members when the reading ended. Instead of questions like "What kind of prayer will be the right one?" or "At what time of day could we all be committed to praying?" the group members wondered aloud, "Where do you think the attack will come?" Fear had crept in and overshadowed the hopeful promise in Cayce's prophetic statement.

Looking back more than forty years later, we may think of those people as having been foolish or fear ridden. We wonder how they could have missed the spirit of what was being promised, how they could have failed to see and grasp the spiritual opportunity being offered them. And yet don't we often do the same thing now? The principles and numbers are still the same. The situation may be a bit different. World War II has come and gone, but today there are equally threatening prospects for our world. But once again, sixty-four people might be enough to make the difference for a nation the size of America.

So what is our response? Do we wonder where the first earthquake will hit? Do we speculate on what kinds of riots will ensue if there is economic collapse? The opportunity is still there to be the little leaven that quickens the consciousness of the masses. This is a powerful concept which says that a small group of dedicated people can have a tremendous effect on the course of the future. It is an idea that bestows on us a sense of promise and a challenge of responsibility. And we are more likely to feel some hope and accept that responsibility if we see clearly just how the magic of "critical mass" works in the realm of human awareness.

A Mechanism to Explain Critical Mass

How is it that ten righteous people or the prayers of just one individual could save a city? What forces and laws are at work to create such an extraordinary thing? Is it that God is placed in a dilemma? Perhaps in looking down on Sodom and seeing ten righteous people, God would feel "stuck." He could not afford to destroy His best followers, this line of reasoning would say, so He would be forced to let everyone else off the hook.

However attractive this kind of argument may be, it has little merit. It reduces God to a befuddled being who dishes out punishment and yet is easily manipulated and cornered. We can do far better than this lame and naive explanation of how the principle of critical mass works on human consciousness. We can identify the universal laws that are at work and that naturally govern this process.

Let's begin with the universal law of oneness, which Cayce proposed as the most fundamental principle in the universe. In fact, one Cayce reading says that the law of oneness is so fundamental to the way the cosmos runs that it should be the object of study for the first *six months* of spiritual inquiry. We might wonder how we could ever study that law for so long. It seems as if we could merely agree that all force or energy is essentially just an expression of the one life force. Then we could move on to more interesting topics. However, there is much more than this to the notion of oneness. There are many subtle ways in which it directs our experiences.

For example, the law of oneness provides us with a clue about how a threshold number of people can change the course of the future for all humanity. It's a key to understanding a mechanism that may allow the love of a few people to lift the awareness of humanity. The law of oneness begins by asserting that there are not two equal but opposing powers of good and evil that are battling for dominion of human minds. There is light and there is darkness, yes. Our experience tells us this, and no abstract law of oneness can deny this experience which we all have. There are good works being done by some people, and there are evil-appearing, destructive works being done by others. The question, however, is this: What's the relationship between them, between light and darkness, or good and evil? Are they *equal* but opposing powers? If so, then we have majority rule when they clash, and nine units of good when confronted with ten units of evil will always result in a victory for evil.

But is that really what happens? When light confronts darkness, what is the result of their interaction? For example, if someone lights a candle in a darkened auditorium, doesn't the light permeate the entire room? Admittedly, that candle may illuminate the huge room with only a very dim light, but the fact remains that the darkness does not overpower the tiny candle flame. Light and darkness are not really equal but opposing forces. Darkness is better understood as an absence of light.

In other words, there is a fundamental oneness in the elements of this example. There is the one force, which in its full manifestation is pure light. It's possible to experience diminished or dimmed expressions of that one force—or even the absence of its expression. But the darkness is not a power that is independent of the light and could defeat it by superior numbers.

In the same fashion, the prayers of one person can work to save an entire community. The darkened consciousnesses of thousands of people do not constitute a power that can defeat a lighted prayer, despite numerical superiority. Of course, that one person who lives in a community of fear and selfishness may be psychologically affected by her surroundings. She may feel discouraged, drained and stuck in the thinking patterns of her neighbors. She may forget to pray or may doubt the value of prayer. In this sense the darkness can "win." However, the law of oneness holds that once that person remembers to pray and believes that healing work is being done, then the darkened consciousness of the masses does not block the widespread impact.

In addition to the law of oneness, a second universal law helps us to understand the mechanism of critical mass. It's a principle from physics: the law of resonance. Perhaps you recall from high school physics the way in which tuning forks can demonstrate this law at a physical level. What happens if you strike a tuning fork and set it to vibrating and then move it near another fork of similar structure? It will set the second tuning fork to vibrating as well. Something similar happens at the level of human minds. It may well be that the vibration of consciousness can have a resonant effect upon other minds, recreating a sympathetic vibration or state of awareness.

Let's consider two ways in which the law of resonance may

operate to explain the critical mass effect on human minds and behavior. First, consider an idea that Cayce and many others have suggested. Is it possible that there are many souls of advanced spiritual development who stand ready to help the earth in this time of transition? This aid may be through direct incarnation if appropriate parents can be found, or it may be through the infusion of ideas and knowledge which could be telepathically transferred (perhaps even without the receiver being quite sure where that inspirational insight came from!). These ideas might be philosophical insights into the human condition, or they might be technological inventions which could help humanity deal with threatened physical survival. The law of resonance would give us one way of understanding how this assistance would be received. If a certain number of people made themselves into receptive tuning forks of the proper structure, then they might be set to "vibrating" with a conscious awareness that is quite extraordinary.

What if instead of philosophical and technological ideas being transferred to receptive channels, it was certain vibratory frequencies of energy itself. The reception and expression of such energies might be used to heal physical bodies or perhaps even to heal and purify our polluted and sick physical earth. We can only guess at what kind of help might be available from conscious beings in other dimensions of God's creation. Of course, we cannot passively await their intervention and expect them to clear up the mess we have collectively created. However, there may be significant validity to the law of resonance. It probably applies to a lot more than just physical objects like tuning forks. As we work to shape our personal "structure"—by meditation, exercise, diet, etc.—we may some day find ourselves set to vibrating with energies or ideas that seem to come from beyond ourselves and which promise to help the world as a whole.

It could well be that within every person there are many "tuning forks." Each one of these tuning forks symbolizes a distinct outlook on life or a state of mind. (And anyone who seriously studies himself is quick to discover this inner diversity.) According to Cayce's philosophy, one such tuning fork within each and every one of us is special: the extraordinary state of mind he called the universal Christ Consciousness. Perhaps it has been buried away and forgotten in many people, but it's still there. However, it can be activated in one of two ways. The first is by conscious effort on the part of the individual—by seeking it out and making specific efforts to mobilize its vibration in physical life. It's probably safe to say that only a small percentage of the world's population is involved in diligently doing this now.

The second way is by the law of resonance. If someone nearby has set his or her own Christ Consciousness tuning fork to vibrating, it may create a sympathetic activity in similar structures in other people, just as surely as the experiment worked in high school physics class!

And how would people experience such a secondary awakening of Christ Consciousness vibrations? Since they are not voluntarily at work on the spiritual path, how would they receive the new vibrations mysteriously emerging from within themselves? These vibrations might appear as unfamiliar, new feelings about themselves and others. They might come as dreams or intuitions. They could manifest as a change in physical health—for some as a healing and for others as a temporary illness (as the old ways of treating their bodies can no longer be handled by a newly sensitized body and mind). Or they might appear as some sort of cosmic or supernatural physical phenomenon in response to these inner events in man's consciousness. Some people expect an outer, physical reappearance of the Christ—a Second Coming—as the manner in which this global awakening would express itself.

Whatever the means or the appearance, we can expect that some people will be inspired by it. Because of what spontaneously happens to them, they proceed consciously to begin work on *nurturing* this newly realized spiritual dimension of themselves. However, others may be more frightened or stubborn about the process, and they would reject what they feel happening to themselves.

Here, then, is a scenario for how human consciousness will be transformed in the coming decades. It doesn't require the impact of outer earth changes—cataclysms such as earthquakes, wars or weather changes. This interpretation of Cayce's most essential millennium prophecy is much less sensationalistic. It shows how relatively few people could work to bring on a new culture for a new millennium. The key ingredient will be a sufficient number of people dealing creatively with the stress of their own inner millennium shift.

The scenario supposes that even a small group—perhaps only several thousand people—will begin to handle the inner changes in a loving, creative, responsible fashion. These people will not be sucked into the darkened consciousness of the masses, which is cynical and fearful. Instead they will attune themselves; they will make themselves of such a "structure" that new energies and new ideas will set their minds and bodies to vibrating through the law of resonance. They will receive aid from the Christ Consciousness within themselves and perhaps also from spiritual beings in other dimensions. When the membership of this group reaches a certain number, then a critical mass point will have been reached—a threshold level will have been achieved and a tremendous new effect will come into play.

Now a second type of resonance will be set in motion throughout the planet. Perhaps within a matter of months—although it could be years—resonant vibrations will begin to stir to life the Christ Consciousness. It will happen in people of all faith traditions, and each person will find words out of their own cultural context to describe it. Even those who haven't been seeking inwardly or spiritually will begin spontaneously to have transformative experiences. This will be a remarkable event in human history. It will be a moment when humanity is on the verge of a quantum leap in awareness.

If that moment coincides with a period of catastrophic outer changes in the world, then the choices and responses will be even more crucial. But this scenario supposes that very large numbers of people will be inspired by the new ideas that they feel coming from within themselves. Remarkable dreams, intuitions and feelings will come to millions, even many of those who haven't been consciously seeking them. Certainly there will be holdouts, individuals who may fearfully hold on to the old ways. But we'll have turned the corner, and the momentum will have become unstoppable. Humanity will be at the dawn of what Cayce and so many others have predicted for the twenty-first century and beyond— a new paradigm for human living based on cooperation and peace.

The Politics of the Transition

It has been said that politicians are the last to respond to changes in mass consciousness. The spirit of the times is usually felt in art, science and religion before it finds expression in the power games of the governing process. How, then, we might wonder, will the transition to a new paradigm overcome the blocks created by world leaders who want to hang on to the old system? How can enlightened souls have an impact on the decisions being made which affect all nations?

There is no point in claiming that by magic several thousand spiritually attuned people can cause world leaders to alter the quality and direction of their decisions. Instead of relying on magic for an explanation, let us consider by what mechanism spiritually attuned people can create what Cayce envisioned as an "invisible empire." Speaking in 1927 of those who might dedicate their lives to an expression of the universal Christ Spirit, Cayce called such individuals "those that would *build* an invisible empire within the hearts of men" (#3976–4).

The term "empire" is a blatantly political one. It refers to power and influence in human affairs that extend beyond the borders of any one nation. Historically, we might think of the Roman Empire or the Persian Empire, clear examples of political influences that spanned many regions and nationalities. When the Cayce readings refer to spiritually attuned people creating an invisible empire, they suggest that we can influence the decision-making process that governs the nations. And "invisible" suggests that the influence will come at the levels of mind and spirit.

But how can we really have an effect upon the decisions that shape the world—such as the choices of war and peace, or the decisions on how national resources will be spent? The answer lies in first considering who it is that is really in control of the world.

Before you respond that it's the presidents of the United States and Russia, or the chairmen of Exxon and I.T.T., think about this principle: *only those who can truly control themselves can claim to control things beyond themselves.* That means control over one's body, attitudes, emotions and actions. And the indisputable evidence is that most, if not all, of the so-called world leaders are actually controlled. This isn't a matter of some conspiracy in which multinational corporations secretly mold the decisions of governments. Instead it's a matter of world leaders not being enlightened, spiritually free beings. And so, they are controlled, but the influence comes from their own subconscious minds. Their desires, fears, insecurities, and habits shape the nature of their decisions which, in turn, affect millions of people. Often those controlling influences from within themselves are hidden or only dimly perceived.

Imagine, for example, how many important decisions are made by world leaders because of a feeling, mood or hunch. Suppose a national leader had to decide the next morning whether or not to invade a neighboring country. Consider but one factor: the quality and content of his or her dreams that night (remembered or unremembered) will likely leave that world leader with a particular mood or perspective in the morning, which could have a large effect upon the decision.

To the degree that world leaders are not yet enlightened beings who are free from the controlling influence of their own subconscious minds, we can exert a tremendous impact on their decisions. It is at the level of the subconscious mind that the apparent decision makers are directable. If Cayce is correct and all subconscious minds *are* in contact with one another, then we have identified a vehicle for creating an invisible empire. From a dimension beyond the three-dimensional physical world, enlightened awareness has an influence. A world leader may never say, "I feel people praying for me and encouraging me to select the way of cooperation and peace." However, that may be exactly what is taking place.

In the past, patterns of fear or confusion may have existed within the subconscious mind of that leader which exerted a control and which led to choices of international tension and discord. But in the not-too-distant future, that same subconscious level may be the avenue by which the world leader is led to see matters a bit differently or to have new feelings and hunches about how to deal with old problems.

We can make a difference in the shaping of world events. We can make *the* difference. Just look at the arithmetic that can be extrapolated from some of the Cayce prophecies. Sixty-four people were once enough to change the destiny of the United States, a nation of 150 million people at the time. We could use the same ratios of influence applied to the modern *world* population of 5.5 billion. That would give us approximately 2400 as a target number for the critical mass to change the destiny of humanity. Perhaps as few as just 2400 people who truly live and pray in attunement with God's plan will be the threshold amount to trigger global changes for healing.

If we will just understand the power to which we have access, this can occur. If we will but look deeply and see what power is really all about, then we can judge in whose hands it actually lies. Yes, we can make the difference. By the way that a few of us prepare for and deal with the inner aspect of the millennium changes, we will largely determine what form the outer millennium changes will take. Just a handful of spiritually dedicated people can create a graceful, loving form of change in which all humanity will participate. And that, at its core, is the fundamental millennium prophecy of Edgar Cayce.

ABOUT THE AUTHOR

Mark Thurston, Ph.D., is an administrator, psychologist, and author of more books on the Cayce readings than any other writer. His fifteen books cover virtually all the aspects of Cayce's approach to spiritual disciplines, soul growth, human relations, and how we help to shape the future. His leadership role with the Cayce material includes his current position as Executive Director of the Association for Research and Enlightenment, an international research and membership organization founded by Cayce in 1931.

Dr. Thurston's previous book is now widely recognized as the best explanation of Cayce's creative psychology for living in these times of extraordinary change: *The Edgar Cayce Handbook for Creating Your Future*. Coauthored with Christopher Fazel, it does not deal specifically with any of the Cayce prophecies, but it examines the specific ways in which each of us can take direct responsibility for shaping our personal and collective futures.

Among his other significant publications are two highly practical guidebooks to dream study: *How to Interpret Your Dreams* and *Dreams: Tonight's Answers for Tomorrow's Questions*. Thousands of readers have been helped to find greater meaning in their vocations through his two books *Discovering Your Soul's Purpose* and *Soul Purpose: Discovering and Fulfilling Your Destiny.*

His innovative book on decision making, choice, and free will, *Paradox of Power: Balancing Personal and Higher Will,* has been acclaimed as one of the finest treatments ever of this complex topic that is so critical to healthy human growth and spiritual development.

Dr. Thurston has been married for sixteen years to Mary Elizabeth Lynch, a practicing attorney. They work and reside in Virginia Beach, Virginia, with their two children.

THE WORK OF EDGAR CAYCE CONTINUES

In the more than fifty years since Cayce's death, the organization he founded in 1931 has continued his efforts in helping people to understand the purpose of life, the role of psychic awareness, and other mysteries of the mind. You can get free information about the Association for Research and Enlightenment (A.R.E.) in Virginia Beach, Virginia, by calling its headquarters: 1-800-333-4499.

The A.R.E. sponsors conferences and lectures throughout the U.S. and Canada on many aspects of Cayce's work—the potentials of the mind, how to use intuition and dreams in daily life decision making, the mind-body-spirit connection in healing, in addition to many other topics addressed in the Cayce material. A considerable portion of the Cayce readings deal with a holistic perspective of health and the healing process.

The A.R.E. Headquarters—where visitors are always welcome—includes one of the finest specialized libraries to be found anywhere in the world. Its sixty thousand volume collection includes hundreds of titles related to developing psychic ability, dream psychology, intuition, reincarnation, destiny and free will, the purpose of life, and the universal laws that shape our lives.

For those who choose to become a member of the A.R.E.—joining a worldwide network of tens of thousands—additional resources are also available. The organization maintains a list of health care professionals who are interested in applying the Cayce approach. Members can borrow detailed collections of what Cayce had to say about specific medical and nonmedical subjects—more than four hundred different collections have been compiled and are available. You'll find fascinating subjects and life-changing ideas on a wide range of themes: psychic awareness, prophecy, reincarnation, meditation, spirituality, vocational guidance, ESP, intuition, and dozens more. Members also receive a magazine *Venture Inward* which includes columnists and feature articles on how to transform one's own life using spiritual principles.

The A.R.E. offers study groups in most cities, many local regional activities, an international tours program, a retreat-type camp for children and adults, and A.R.E. contacts around the world. The Cayce materials also form an integral part of Atlantic University (also in Virginia Beach, Virginia) which offers a master's degree in Transpersonal Studies, with options to specialize in several areas such as intuitive studies, holistic health, and the visual arts.

For free information about any or all of these programs, call the toll-free number listed on the previous page, write to A.R.E., 67th and Atlantic Ave., Box 595, Virginia Beach, VA 23451-0595; or visit our website at http//:www.are-cayce.com on the worldwide web.